At Issue

|Fast Food

Other Books in the At Issue Series:

At Issue

Fast Food

Tamara Thompson, Book Editor

GREENHAVEN PRESS
A part of Gale, Cengage Learning

Farmington Hills, Mich • San Francisco • New York • Waterville, Maine
Meriden, Conn • Mason, Ohio • Chicago

GALE
CENGAGE Learning

Patricia Coryell, *Vice President & Publisher, New Products & GVRL*
Douglas Dentino, *Manager, New Products*
Judy Galens, *Acquisitions Editor*

© 2015 Greenhaven Press, a part of Gale, Cengage Learning.

WCN: 01-100-101

Gale and Greenhaven Press are registered trademarks used herein under license.

For more information, contact:
Greenhaven Press
27500 Drake Rd.
Farmington Hills, MI 48331-3535
Or you can visit our Internet site at gale.cengage.com

For product information and technology assistance, contact us at

Gale Customer Support, 1-800-877-4253
For permission to use material from this text or product, submit all requests online at www.cengage.com/permissions.

Further permissions questions can be e-mailed to permissionrequest@cengage.com.

Articles in Greenhaven Press anthologies are often edited for length to meet page requirements. In addition, original titles of these works are changed to clearly present the main thesis and to explicitly indicate the author's opinion. Every effort is made to ensure that Greenhaven Press accurately reflects the original intent of the authors. Every effort has been made to trace the owners of copyrighted material.

Cover photograph copyright © Images.com/Corbis.

LIBRARY OF CONGRESS CATALOGING-IN-PUBLICATION DATA

Fast food / Tamara Thompson, book editor.
    pages cm. -- (At issue)
    Includes bibliographical references and index.
    ISBN 978-0-7377-7165-7 (hardcover) -- ISBN 978-0-7377-7166-4 (pbk.)
    1. Convenience foods--United States. 2. Fast food restaurants--United States. 3. Food industry and trade--United States. I. Thompson, Tamara.
    TX370.F372 2015
    642'.10973--dc23
                                                            2014047300

Printed in the United States of America
2 3 4 5 6   19 18 17 16 15

Contents

Introduction

There are few things as quintessentially American as a fast food meal. Born from a few start-up burger places serving southern California's car culture and riding the expansion of the interstate highway system in the 1950s, the fast food industry has since grown to fill a niche like no other in American history.

"The extraordinary growth of the fast food industry has been driven by fundamental changes in American society,"[1] writes Eric Schlosser in his seminal book on the topic, *Fast Food Nation: The Dark Side of the All-American Meal*. Those changes included the rise of automobile ownership and the adoption of mechanized processes, but especially the phenomenon of women entering the workforce and leaving behind such traditional roles as shopping and meal preparation.

"A generation ago," writes Schlosser, "three-quarters of the money used to buy food in the United States was spent to prepare meals at home. Today about half of the money used to buy food is spent at restaurants—mainly at fast food restaurants."[2]

In 1970, Americans spent about $6 billion on fast food; in 2014, fast food sales were projected to be more than $195 billion, according to Statista, a web-based statistics company that serves a wide range of industries. "The US fast food industry remains the largest in the world, with over 320,000 outlets forecast to be operating in 2014,"[3] Statista notes. According to

1. Eric Schlosser, *Fast Food Nation: The Dark Side of the All-American Meal*. New York: Houghton Mifflin Co., 2001.
2. Ibid.
3. Statista, "Revenue of the United States Fast Food Restaurant Industry from 2002 to 2018," Statista: The Statistics Portal, 2014. http://www.statista.com/statistics/196614 /revenue-of-the-us-fast-food-restaurant-industry-since-2002.

a 2013 Gallup poll, eight in ten Americans report eating fast food at least once a month, with almost half saying they eat it at least once a week.

As much as American culture shaped the demand for fast food, however, so too has the culture been transformed by it. According to Schlosser, "over the last three decades, fast food has infiltrated every nook and cranny of American society" and has become nothing less than "a revolutionary force in American life."[4]

For millions, fast food restaurants are the source of positive associations with birthday parties, play dates, and ubiquitously predictable and accessible comfort food. For others, they represent first paychecks, a lifeline meal on a busy day, or the secret to quieting a cranky toddler on a long car trip. Still others, however, equate fast food with dead-end jobs and near-poverty wages, cultural homogenization and economic predation, or serious health issues such as obesity and diabetes.

Such disparate views mean that it's impossible to talk about fast food without also talking about public health, politics, profit, and even environmental sustainability.

The massive purchasing power of the fast food industry makes it one of the most powerful industries in the world and inextricably links it to the national economy, to millions of American jobs, to the stock market, and to the interests of powerful multinational corporations like agribusiness giants Monsanto and Cargill.

Fast food influences US agricultural policies, the living conditions of cows and chickens in factory farms, the accepted practices in slaughterhouses, and governmental oversight of food safety. It shapes global public health statistics and helps determine the price of eggs, the cost of dinner, and consumer attitudes about mass consumption.

4. Op. cit.

"What people eat (or don't eat) has always been determined by a complex interplay of social, economic, and technological forces,"[5] writes Schlosser, and that has perhaps never been more true than when it comes to fast food.

Fast food is quite literally the lynchpin of the industrial food system in the United States and, increasingly, the global one. Today's fast food chains sit at the top of the proverbial food pyramid, directly or indirectly shaping everything that goes on below them—from the number and type of potatoes farmers plant in Idaho, to the acres of Amazon Rainforest lost to cattle grazing each year, to the availability of fresh food in inner city communities.

"During a relatively brief period of time, the fast food industry has helped to transform not only the American diet, but also our landscape, economy, workforce, and popular culture," writes Schlosser. "Fast food and its consequences have become inescapable, regardless of whether you eat it twice a day, try to avoid it, or have never taken a single bite."[6]

The authors in *At Issue: Fast Food* consider a wide range of viewpoints related to the health, environmental, economic, and social impacts of fast food, both in the United States and elsewhere as this quintessentially American creation is exported around the globe.

5. Op. cit.
6. Op. cit.

1

Fast Food Is Harmful to People and the Planet

Food Empowerment Project

The Food Empowerment Project is a California-based nonprofit that works to create a more just and sustainable world by recognizing the power of individuals' food choices.

Because of its heavy reliance on products that are high in sugar, fat, and calories, the fast food industry is a major force behind skyrocketing health problems and obesity in humans. The unhealthy factory farming practices that cheap fast food depends on are cruel to animals and unsustainable for the planet because they degrade the environment and contribute to global warming. There is also a serious problem with worker wage exploitation and injury in the fast food industry. Because of the massive worldwide reach and influence of the fast food industry, these problems are not small or limited in scope; they are a global crisis. Fast food is harmful to public health, workers, animals, and the environment.

Fast food in the U.S. has grown from a $6 billion-a-year industry in 1970 into a corporate juggernaut with more than $170 billion in annual revenues today. Especially because "meat," dairy and eggs are the main ingredients in fast food, the exponential increase in its consumption has engendered a wide range of negative social impacts—including rapidly rising diet-related disease rates, worker exploitation, systemic animal abuse, and environmental degradation.

The fast food industry's economic clout has not only enabled it to affect a radical shift in the country's eating patterns, but also fundamentally alter the very way that food is produced. The industry's enormous purchasing power and demand for vast amounts of cheap animal products are among the principle driving forces behind factory farming, as well as the massive government subsidies for staple animal feed crops like corn and soy that sustain it. As a result of the industry's excessive economic influence, gigantic multinational corporations like McDonalds, Burger King and KFC make huge profits selling fast food at artificially-reduced prices.

Companies deliberately whet children's appetite for fast food through age-specific advertising campaigns.

Meanwhile, obscured behind the veneer of fast food companies' slick multi-billion-dollar marketing campaigns are the true costs to public health, fast food workers, animal welfare, and the environment.

Fast Food and Dietary Diseases

Volumes of peer-reviewed scientific studies conclusively correlate the consumption of "meat" and other animal products with many of the deadliest medical disorders plaguing humankind today, including cardiovascular disease, cancer, diabetes, and obesity. The overall U.S. obesity rate has more than doubled since 1980, with more than two-thirds of adults and about one-fifth of all children now being overweight or obese. Both nutritional researchers and public health agencies implicate fast food as a major contributor to the obesity epidemic, mainly because of its high sugar, fat and calorie content (and low overall nutritional value).

Children who consume fast food eat more calories overall than those who do not (either regularly or on particular days) because these low-fiber "empty calories" leave people hungry later. One study found that kids who eat fast food consume an average of about 15 percent more calories than those who do not, and gain about an extra six pounds per year as a result if they do not burn those excess calories off through exercise. Fast food was also the main food source for 29 to 38 percent of the randomly-chosen subjects in this study, and it typically replaced healthier options like fresh fruits and vegetables in their diets.

Companies deliberately whet children's appetite for fast food through age-specific advertising campaigns, including television commercials for "Happy Meals" with movie tie-in toys for younger kids and smartphone promotions and online games aimed at teens. Given that fast food companies now collectively spend over $4 billion a year on advertising (with at least $1.5 billion of that directly targeting children), it is no surprise that kids six to eleven years of age were exposed to 59 percent more Subway ads, 26 percent more McDonalds ads, and 10 percent more Burger King ads in 2009 than they were in 2007. Another study by researchers at Yale University found that companies even target young consumers by ethnicity, with African Americans being exposed to at least 50 percent more fast food advertisements than white children and teens.

Fast Food and the "Obesogenic Environment"

Research shows that, in low-income areas and communities of color especially, fast food franchises tend to cluster around schools, further extending their marketing outreach to young people. This contributes to an "Obesogenic Environment" in which close proximity to fast foods (often at the expense of access to healthier options) increases their consumption of these products—along with the girth of their waistlines.

A similar pattern of fast food concentration is also generally found throughout low-income areas and communities of color, where there are on average 30 percent fewer supermarkets than in middle- and high-income regions, which coincides with the results found in Food Empowerment's report, "Shining a Light on the Valley of Heart's Delight." The high density of fast food outlets (as well as liquor and convenience stores) in these neighborhoods selling cheap high-calorie foods often crowds out supermarkets, grocery stores and farmers markets that offer healthy (but often more expensive) dietary options. This results in the proliferation of "food deserts" where residents have little or no access to fresh produce, whole grains and unprocessed foods.

It is clear fast food corporations don't care about anybody—not the workers, not the animals, not the environment, and of course not people's health.

Food Deserts

African-Americans, Latinos and other people of color most likely to live in food deserts suffer disproportionately from higher rates of obesity (and therefore other diet-related disorders) than whites—and fast food is one of the main causes of this deadly disparity. Residents of food deserts typically have a plethora of fast food restaurants to choose from within walking distance of their homes, but the nearest supermarket or grocery store may be miles away, and many low-income individuals do not have access to private transportation and must work two jobs just to make ends meet. Feeding their families fast food is therefore usually quicker, easier and less expensive than shopping for and preparing home-cooked meals. However, reliance on fast food as a dietary staple (especially over long periods of time) causes dangerously unhealthy weight gain and other physical problems resulting from poor nutrition.

Fast Food Impacts on Workers, Animals and the Environment

In addition to harming human health, the fast food industry also has detrimental impacts on:

- *Workers*: At any given time, there are about 3.5 million fast food workers in the U.S. They typically work for minimum wage without medical benefits or the right to unionize, so turnover is extremely high. With the agricultural industry ranking as one of the most hazardous industries to work for in the U.S., fast food workers, however, also suffer one of the highest injury rates of any employment sector, and are statistically more likely than police officers to be murdered while working.

- *Animals*: Since fast food companies purchase such a large proportion of the "meat," dairy and eggs produced by farmers, they are able to exert enormous influence over how animals are raised for food. As a result, factory farms supply the fast food industry's demand for vast volumes of animal products at the lowest possible cost by crowding animals together to conserve space (often confining them in cages or crates), pumping them full of non-therapeutic antibiotics and artificial growth hormones, amputating body parts to avoid unnatural stress-induced injuries, and slaughtering them at breakneck speeds on mechanized disassembly lines (often while they remain fully conscious). Cows, chickens and pigs raised to make fast food endure lifelong pain and suffering on factory farms where they are treated like interchangeable production units.

- *The Environment*: According to a landmark report by the United Nations' Food and Agriculture Organization, the livestock sector (and factory farming in particular) is "one of the top two or three most significant contributors to the most serious environmental problems, at every scale from local to global the world faces today." Meanwhile, fast food companies jointly profit more from factory farming than perhaps any other commercial or industrial sector. In addition, millions of acres of forest are clear-cut every year to manufacture fast food packaging, which comprises approximately one-fifth of all litter in the U.S. In addition, to prevent grease leakage, many fast food companies coat their paper packaging with perfluoroalkyls, which are toxic compounds that harm the environment and human health.

It is clear fast food corporations don't care about anybody—not the workers, not the animals, not the environment, and of course not people's health. It's all about making a profit. We would like to tell people not to buy from these fast food giants, but we know that might not always be possible. When there is no choice it is still possible to make a difference by making sure to ask for a vegan option.

2

Some Fast Food Chains Work Toward Sustainability

Barney Wolf

Barney Wolf is an Ohio-based freelancer for QSR Magazine, *a trade publication for the $268 billion "quick-serve" restaurant industry.*

Despite the generally poor environmental reputation of the fast food industry, many fast food chains are actually working very hard to make their business practices more sustainable. Some of the largest "quick-serve" chains, as the industry calls them, are using meat raised by specific standards of environmental stewardship and humane animal care. Some examples are chains that use only "free-range" eggs, meats that are free of hormones or steroids, cattle that have been pasture raised and fed grass instead of grain in a crowded feed lot, or seafood certified by the Marine Stewardship Council. When big corporations make significant changes like that, it can have a profound impact not only on the fast food industry but on the welfare of the planet itself.

Sustainable practices are all the rage across the restaurant industry these days.

The expansive show floors at the National Restaurant Association's annual trade show in May confirmed that the momentum behind these initiatives isn't waning. From tableware and takeout containers to faucets, lighting, and cleaning products, green was the word. That also extends to the proteins most quick-service and fast-casual restaurants use as their menuboard centerpieces.

The concept of creating and maintaining a sustainable food supply has been embraced in varying degrees by a growing number of restaurant operations, ranging from Atlanta's two-unit Yeah! Burger to giant, worldwide chains like McDonald's.

"Sustainability is everything to us," says Erik Maier, chief executive and founder of Yeah! Burger. "I started the company because I wanted there to be more sustainable options for people. Our message has resonated."

Defining *sustainability* can be challenging. Most believe it refers to the practices that meet resource needs without harming the ability to meet future demands. But determining how to accomplish that requires more study.

There are many pillars that contribute to sustainability, including people, communities, animal welfare, social welfare, the environment, innovation, and food safety and supply.

Take the Global Roundtable for Sustainable Beef (GRSB), consisting of major agricultural, environmental, and restaurant experts, as well as other stakeholders. It was formed a few years ago to foster a sustained beef supply as the world's population continues to grow.

Defining Sustainability Is Difficult

One of the organization's goals this year is to define the term *sustainability*.

"That's a big question," says Ruaraidh Petre, the Netherlands-based executive director of the GRSB. "We don't claim to have all the answers. Anyone you ask about sustainability in the beef industry will have a different opinion."

There are many pillars that contribute to sustainability, including people, communities, animal welfare, social welfare, the environment, innovation, and food safety and supply. The GRSB won't take a position on some issues, like grass versus grain cattle feed, because both are represented in the organization. "There is room for improvement in every system," Petre says.

One Roundtable member, McDonald's, is "an enthusiastic supporter of the GRSB and their multi-stakeholder, science-based, holistic approach," says Bob Langert, the company's vice president of corporate sustainability, in a statement.

McDonald's has in recent years pushed its beef providers toward more sustainable actions, both in animal welfare and environmental management practices.

Yeah! Burger and some additional newer burger chains have focused on sustainability since they opened their doors.

"We wanted our signature product to be as sustainable as possible," Maier says. "That's why we went out and found a local supplier (White Oak Pastures), who is hands down one of the most humane farms in the country, and it's three-and-a-half hours south of Atlanta."

Atlanta is also the home of Farm Burger, which has four units in Georgia and North Carolina. Its beef is from the chain's own cooperative of small, grass-fed, grass-finished cattle producers.

Good Flavor and Good Karma Too

"It can be tricky managing it," owner George Frangos says. "We've had to grow our co-op as we've grown, because there's no other constant supply of what we want," which is cattle that is never fed antibiotics, hormones, or grain.

Grass-fed beef's taste led Dean Loring to choose that ingredient for his Southern California restaurant chain, Burger Lounge.

"I'm an S.O.B.—son of a butcher—and what I really like about grass-fed beef even more than its sustainability and healthfulness is the flavor," he says. "This is what beef tasted like before the agri-corn industry began fattening cattle with things foreign to their diets."

The higher cost to raise [grass-fed] cattle pushes up burger prices by about $1 per item at these restaurants.

Chicago's Epic Burger, meanwhile, has opted for grain-fed beef, but only from cattle that are humanely raised without hormones or antibiotics.

"No cooped-up cows on drugs," says the chain's founder, David Friedman. "We want to make sure the animals live a happy, healthy life. The food tastes better, and there's better karma all around."

The higher cost to raise these types of cattle pushes up burger prices by about $1 per item at these restaurants.

It's not just burger places that use grass-fed, no-hormone beef. Moe's Southwest Grill also uses the product for its steak and has been transitioning to an all-natural product over the past year.

"We want to focus on our food mission: no transfats, no microwaves in any stores, no products containing MSG, and we definitely don't want to add hormones to our proteins," says Carmisha McKenzie, the Atlanta-based chain's [research and development] culinary manager. Grass-fed beef "definitely allows the cattle to grow in a more natural environment."

What About Chicken?

Beef has long been the key protein for quick serves, and that continues today, as three of the top five U.S. operators primarily serve burgers. But per-capita consumption of beef has declined and chicken has taken over the top spot among consumers.

Many restaurant operators no longer use meat or eggs from chickens confined in tight cages, and federal rules ban hormone use in raising any fowl. But more humane treatment doesn't necessarily correspond with sustainability. Free-range chickens, which must have access to the outdoors, are more sustainable if they can be in pastures with a more natural life cycle. Even better, some experts say, are chickens raised on grass pastures most of their lives.

"A pastured model is often part of a larger grazing system a farmer may have," says Mike Badger, director of the American Pastured Poultry Producers Association.

This model uses a managed rotational system like "day ranging," with a large shelter that is moved every few days, giving chickens access to different areas of a pasture. The birds feed on grass, weeds, bugs, and some grains and leave naturally fertilizing manure.

Among the restaurants that use day-ranged chicken are Rick Bayless's collection of restaurants in Chicago, including the fast casuals Xoco and Frontera Grill.

A number of restaurants, like Farm Burger, don't use pastured poultry but still opt for chicken raised humanely and without antibiotics or growth additives. "Pastured poultry really can't supply enough, and the cost jump is really high," Frangos says. "We feel good where we are."

Free-range turkey is not always easy to procure, either. Epic Burger's Friedman, for one, says he has been unable to find a reliable all-natural turkey supply.

Burger Lounge, on the other hand, has taken advantage of a large Southern California farm for the free-range birds in the chain's turkey burgers, which are "a large seller," Loring says.

The Chipotle Model

Chipotle has been a leader in moving limited-service restaurants toward more natural and sustainable proteins. It began in the late 1990s, when founder Steve Ells was looking for methods to improve the taste of the chain's carnitas. He was horrified by the crowded pig feeding operations and decided to begin sourcing from natural pork producers, says Chris Arnold, spokesman for Chipotle. Now "all of our meat is naturally raised in a humane way, without antibiotics or hormones," he says.

The American pork industry is intent on improving sustainability and has made considerable strides toward that goal.

Some operators procure pork from producers who raise their livestock in pastures. At Sloco in Nashville, most of the meat comes from farms less than 200 miles away.

"We are completely focused on sustainable food and making sustainable food, particularly proteins, more affordable," says Sloco owner Jeremy Chase Barlow. The restaurant uses entire pigs for its sandwiches, including ham, bacon, pork loin, and pulled pork, plus corned pork shoulders in the Redneck Reuben.

The American pork industry is intent on improving sustainability and has made considerable strides toward that goal, says Allan Stokes, director of environmental programs for the National Pork Board. The industry recently conducted a 50-year retrospective and has managed to "lower its land footprint by 56 percent, based on pounds of pork produced," he says. "It's 41 percent lower for water, and the carbon footprint has been reduced by 56 percent."

Less-Used Proteins

While beef, chicken, and pork are the proteins used most in limited-service restaurants, some concepts are introducing less-used proteins. Yeah! Burger has bison as a regular burger, and specials like organic lamb, salmon burgers, and shrimp po' boys. Burger Lounge has a "Game Changer" series of limited-time offers, including bison, boar, elk, and lamb.

Lamb is a good sustainable protein option because it's all pasture- or forage-based, says Megan Wortman, executive director of the American Lamb Board. "With more consumers wanting a grass-fed product, we see lamb as a growing segment," she says.

Craig Rogers raises several thousand lambs at his farm near Patrick Springs, Virginia, and supplies a number of restaurants around the eastern half of the country, including some limited-service brands.

"We also make an all-lamb gyro loaf," he says. "Most of the gyro meat in the U.S. is made with a combination of lamb and beef to make it cheaper, but ours uses only lamb."

Among the restaurants he supplies is the Richmond, Virginia, unit of Alabama-based Taziki's Mediterranean Café, which has 26 locations in nine states. The chain uses lamb in two gyros, and it's also grilled as part of a combination meal. The prices are $1 higher at the Richmond unit, and there's no plan to expand that lamb product to the chain's other units.

"The lamb is incredible," says Keith Richards, Taziki's founder, of Rogers' product. "But a lot of it for us is the bottom line, the cost. With this type of lamb, it can get expensive."

McDonald's has pointed to the Filet-O-Fish as the product in which the company has made the greatest strides toward assuring the sustainability of its supply.

Sustainable Seafood

Sustainability is also a major consideration when sourcing seafood. Industrial fishing practices have caused concern about the viability of some species.

For its Filet-O-Fish sandwich, McDonald's sources all of its fish supply from Marine Stewardship Council (MSC)-certified fisheries, says Jon Rump, a spokesman for the company.

"Many fisheries contribute to our supply, but each is MSC certified," he says in an e-mail. McDonald's has pointed to the Filet-O-Fish as the product in which the company has made the greatest strides toward assuring the sustainability of its supply.

Sustainability is important when it comes to the fish used at Fusian, a four-unit fast-casual sushi chain based in Cincinnati.

"It starts out with our suppliers and making sure we know and trust them," says Stephan Harman, cofounder of the brand. "We try to learn the story of our food and communicate that to our guests. We are trying to do the right thing."

Tuna is the most popular protein for Fusian's sushi, and the company works with a Japanese supplier who obtains the fish only from longline fishing sources, which is considered a more sustainable method than using nets.

Vegetarian Options

Of course, some of the most sustainable proteins don't have meat. One of those is tofu, which is served at numerous limited-service restaurants, including Moe's and Chipotle. Hummus, made of mashed chickpeas, is also growing in popularity.

Yeah! Burger has a vegetarian burger made primarily from organic red peas from South Carolina, while Burger Lounge features an organic quinoa veggie burger and Sloco offers a quinoa meatball sub, veggie sandwich with a tofu spread, and seitan.

The seitan, or wheat gluten, is "made into a loaf, braised, and then shaved," Barlow says.

At Epic Burger, which has a portobello mushroom burger, there's an effort to create Mushroom Monday, based on the Meatless Monday movement.

"I know it sounds contradictory, but this would help sustain cattle ranching for a longer period of time and reduce our carbon footprint," Friedman says. "It's probably our biggest contribution to sustainability."

3

Fast Food Chains Had Better Move Past Value Meals and Embrace Health

Hank Cardello

Hank Cardello is director of the Obesity Solutions Initiative at the Hudson Institute, a Washington, DC-based conservative think tank. He is the author of Stuffed: An Insider's Look at Who's (Really) Making America Fat.

The tactics traditionally used by the fast food industry to increase sales—offering cheap burgers and more bang for the consumer buck—don't work very well anymore. Fast food restaurants are discovering that the best way to attract new customers and boost stagnant sales is to offer healthier menu items alongside the old favorites for which a chain is known. More people than ever are concerned about eating a healthier diet and they are avoiding items that are high in calories, fat, and sugar. Offering attractive low-calorie options to increasingly health-conscious customers is the next big wave in fast food.

The fast-food industry is engaged in a price war, but this time there aren't likely to be any big winners.

The reason: Nearly a third of U.S. consumers want healthier food, not just cheaper food. Discounted Whoppers and Big Macs alone won't do the trick.

For a $660 billion industry that employs 10% of the U.S. workforce, the stakes are high. Not much has worked to generate growth in recent years. Just 99 cents gets you a junior cheeseburger today at Wendy's, which is battling McDonald's and other chains over lower-price menu options. At Dairy Queen, five dollars buys a relative smorgasbord: sandwich, soft drink, fries, and a hot fudge sundae. Meanwhile McDonald's global same-store sales dropped last October [2012] for the first time since 2003.

Yet several studies suggest that rampant discounting is not likely to greatly lengthen the drive-through line. The first is a recent Harris study of restaurant patrons. It found that while 90% choose a restaurant based on price, "healthy menu items" are also a top motivator for 58%. The second study comes from the Natural Marketing Institute [NMI], which researched and segmented U.S. consumers by their attitudes about the health aspects of food. NMI found that 17% of consumers could be classified as "well-beings," passionate about eating healthier foods and willing to pay more for it. Another 14% are "food actives," who want to eat better but are more price-sensitive. And 21% are "fence sitters," who know they should make healthier choices but are busy and stressed out and need the dining outlet to make it easy for them. Together these three groups make up 52% of restaurant customers, a group too big to ignore.

Lower-calorie menu items are the next big wave, and restaurant operators needn't choose between 100% healthy and belt-busting.

Attracting Health-Conscious Customers

Restaurants can no longer afford to price-slash their way to growth; they must also find innovative ways to attract these health-conscious customers by giving them what they want. If they don't, they will be missing out on the biggest growth opportunity in decades.

But this doesn't mean dropping their most popular items. They don't need to ban burgers and other high-calorie foods to lure in these customers. Indeed, even the "well-beings" occasionally crave something indulgent. Taco Bell didn't give up on tacos when it introduced its Cantina Bell menu, which along with its bargain-priced Doritos-based tacos helped it outperform its peers last year. Dunkin' Donuts didn't jettison cream-filled donuts when it introduced its highly popular turkey sausage breakfast sandwich, which comes in at under 400 calories. Sbarro's reduced-calorie pizza slice is one of its top sellers, but the chain still offers traditional cheese and pepperoni.

Moreover, consider that past growth engines for the restaurant industry posed little threat to their core menu items. The wildly popular combo meals introduced in the 1980s were just a different way of bundling old products. McDonald's introduced its breakfast menu in 1971 after a Santa Barbara, Calif., franchisee invented the Egg McMuffin. Breakfast eventually became McDonald's second most profitable time slot, topped only by lunchtime, and the new breakfast menu did not compete with the burgers and fries.

The Next Big Wave

Like breakfast foods and combo meals, lower-calorie menu items are the next big wave, and restaurant operators needn't choose between 100% healthy and belt-busting. But they should realize that the 48% of customers who don't care about their eating habits are not growing their businesses anymore. They need to change their menus and marketing to woo the other 52%.

Research by my organization, the Hudson Institute, proves that this is where the growth is. We studied sales growth between 2006 and 2011 at 21 U.S. restaurant chains that collectively account for $102 billion in annual revenue, and we found that those that increased their number of lower-calorie servings also increased same-store sales by 5.5%, while those that decreased the number of lower-calorie servings saw same-store sales *decrease* by 5.5%.

Innovative, attractively priced menu items that give more choices to an increasingly health-conscious restaurant patron are the only way to go.

Healthier food is solidly in fashion, even at the drive-through window, so much so that even Americans' long and torrid love affair with the French fry may be cooling. The Hudson Institute study found that servings of fries dipped by 50 million between 2006 and 2011 at fast-food chains where fries accounted for at least 20% of the menu items sold. Servings of lower-calorie beverages also grew four times as fast as sweetened beverages during that same period. For sure, high-calorie menu staples are a long way from dead, but neither are they growing.

A Recipe for Success

So what should restaurant chains be doing now? Here are three ideas:

- Understand the fast-changing health attitudes of consumers. With few exceptions, mostly in the upscale "well-beings" consumer segment, all consumers have some sensitivity to price. The challenge will be to give them healthier foods at good price points. Just as many environmentally conscious car buyers have shunned hybrids with high sticker prices, health-conscious restaurant patrons won't buy healthier menu items if they feel they are being gouged. The magic bullet is healthier, good-tasting food at a price that makes customers, restaurant chains, and franchisees happy. Subway's combo meals, which have helped propel its growth to the largest restaurant chain by number of stores, are an example of a product with the right formula.

- Adopt stealth health. That means *not* trumpeting a food's health benefits, which some diners equate with depriving themselves. The short and ignominious history of McDonald's "McLean Deluxe" is an example of how meals labeled as "diet food" can be a disaster. Vibrant flavors, thoughtful presentation, and quality ingredients matter more. They will appeal to the "food actives," who want to eat better but whose willpower is weaker than the well-beings'.

- Market healthier menu items more aggressively. "Lite" offerings were once banished to a sorry corner on the last page of the menu. The healthier menu items deserve a marquee spot. Cheesecake Factory uses gorgeous photography to play up its "Skinnylicious" menu, which features items like lettuce-wrapped Asian chicken and other dishes at under 600 calories. The food looks every bit as mouth-watering as the chain's 2,500-calorie belly-buster meals. Good marketers invest budget and creativity in their growth brands, and healthier options are where the growth lies.

Innovative, attractively priced menu items that give more choices to an increasingly health-conscious restaurant patron are the only way to go. Restaurants won't thrive by discounting high-calorie products that a growing number of consumers wouldn't buy at any price.

4

Fast Food Options Have Not Actually Gotten Healthier

Barbara Bronson Gray

Barbara Bronson Gray is an award-winning writer and nationally recognized health expert. She is a regular contributor to the HealthDay news service.

Just because there are more items that seem healthy on fast food menus these days, it doesn't mean that the restaurants' offerings are actually any better for their customers. A recent study showed that although the overall number of menu items has grown significantly industry wide, the average calorie count of the food sold has actually not changed very much. A salad may seem healthy, but when it is topped with fried chicken pieces, high-fat creamy dressing, or other high-calorie toppings, it can actually be more unhealthy than a burger. So-called healthy alternatives at fast food restaurants are really not much better at all. The best option is for people to eat at home more often and to avoid fast food altogether.

You'd like a salad? Want some fries with that?

A new study shows that providing more menu options on a fast-food menu doesn't mean the average diner chows down fewer calories.

Researchers found that although there has been a 53 percent increase in the total number of menu offerings over the last 14 years, the average calorie content of foods sold by eight of the major U.S. fast-food chains has not changed much.

Part of the problem is that some of the highest-calorie foods are masquerading as healthy, said Katherine Bauer, lead author of the study and an assistant professor in the department of public health at Temple University, in Philadelphia. "Entree salads, which are increasing in number, can be bad, too. With fried chicken on top and regular dressing, they can have more calories than a burger."

The study, published in the November [2012] issue of the *American Journal of Preventive Medicine*, analyzed menu offerings and their nutritional value from McDonald's, Burger King, Wendy's, Taco Bell, KFC, Arby's, Jack in the Box and Dairy Queen.

A nutrition expert who was not involved with the study agreed with the study findings.

"Fast food may be offering more so-called 'healthy' alternatives but not necessarily fewer calories," said Lona Sandon, an assistant professor of clinical nutrition at the University of Texas Southwestern Medical Center at Dallas.

A recent survey found that 28 percent of adults had fast food two or more times a week, and 40 percent of high school students consume fast food on any given day.

In the last two years studied—2009 and 2010—the average lunch or dinner entree had 453 calories, while the average side dish had 263 calories.

Calorie Counts Have Not Changed Much

While the researchers didn't see a significant change in the median calorie content of entrees and drinks, they found a small increase in the calories found in condiments and desserts.

According to the study authors, fast food accounts for about 15 percent of Americans' calorie intake, up from about 4 percent in the late 1970s. They said that a recent survey found that 28 percent of adults had fast food two or more times a week, and 40 percent of high school students consume fast food on any given day.

"It's not like one fast-food meal is going to be a problem," Bauer said. "But a good proportion of teenagers are eating fast food three to four times a week."

Rather than blaming Americans for a lack of willpower, Bauer said that they're overexposed to places where most of the available options are unhealthy, high-calorie foods. "We've created environments where it's really impossible to succeed," she said.

Data for the study were taken from the University of Minnesota Nutrition Coordinating Center Food and Nutrient Database, which includes menu items available at 22 U.S. fast-food restaurant chains.

The menus included all foods, drinks, desserts and condiments—such as salad dressing, ketchup, mustard, mayonnaise, jelly, salsa, tartar sauce and croutons—for lunch and dinner. Side dishes included french fries, other fried foods, soups and chili, breads, non-fried potatoes, and other foods such as nachos, baked beans and green beans.

Why Do People Eat Too Many Calories?

Sandon said she thinks part of the problem is that people don't understand calories or have a good idea of how many calories they should be taking in every day. "People also tend to overestimate how many calories they burn when they exercise," she added.

Why wouldn't the availability of more healthy food choices create a decrease in the total calories consumed in fast-food restaurants? Sandon said that while posting the calorie numbers are helpful for people who are eager to manage their health and weight, not everyone reacts that way. "Some people want the most calories for their dollar," she said.

Sandon also thinks just the broader range of menu options may be part of the problem. "When people have more choices they may order more," she said.

One limitation of the study, Sandon noted, is that the researchers only included data up to 2010. She said many of the fast-food chains seem to have decreased calorie counts and expanded healthy menu options only in the last two years.

Sandon suggested consumers try to eat home more often. And when they find themselves at a fast-food restaurant, she recommended that they order the smallest size available, even if it's from the children's menu.

"And remember: Just because it's healthful and nutritious, it doesn't mean it doesn't have calories," Sandon said.

5

Fast Food Is Unfairly Blamed for Obesity

Roy T. Bergold Jr.

Following a thirty-two-year career at McDonald's Corporation, Roy T. Bergold Jr. works as a management and marketing consultant for the restaurant industry.

The "quick-serve" restaurant industry—better known to most people as fast food—is taking most of the blame for America's childhood obesity epidemic, not just because of the quality of food it offers but also because of its aggressive marketing to children. Fast food is being unfairly singled out when it is only one small part of the overall problem, however. Parents, schools, and society at large all play important roles in shaping children's diets, lifestyle choices, and attitudes. Marketers can certainly be more responsible in their marketing to children, but parents and schools must take responsibility, too, by setting and enforcing limits and encouraging healthy eating habits.

Childhood obesity is skyrocketing, and quick serves are unfairly getting the blame.

Nobody ever accused Mom or Grandma's cooking of being a prime contributor to childhood obesity. So why blame the quick-service industry? One out of three kids is classified as overweight or obese. And our marketing is getting the blame.

When I was at the big guy [McDonald's], we were extremely aware of our obligation to kids. Sure, we marketed to kids. As [McDonald's founder] Ray Kroc said, if you had $1 to spend on marketing, spend it on kids, because they bring mom and dad. But we tried to play fair. Our commercials were little stories about good and evil solved by Ronald McDonald and ended with the kids and Ronald at a McDonald's. But we never told kids to buy or taste anything. There was strictly no sell language in the ads. We used small portions, like the regular hamburger and small fries. And we never advertised Coca-Cola because of caffeine content. We showed orange drink and shakes.

Our promotions, like the Happy Meal, had one premium per week, encouraging one out of 21 meals at McDonald's. And the premiums were of the highest quality. One of the first times we did glasses, after the promotion started, we found out that there was a slight amount of lead in the paint. It was way under restrictions, but it was decided to recall the glasses out of concern for our customers. Can you imagine what that cost? I was never more proud of my company.

Obesity is a function of what kids eat, how much they eat, and how much exercise they get.

We had a written manual that told the men playing Ronald how to be Ronald—how to interact with kids, correct language, and what to do when certain problems occurred. Again, it was all out of concern for our customers.

So why are quick serves in so much trouble for marketing to kids? First, let's explore the issue.

Many Factors Cause Obesity

Obesity is a function of what kids eat, how much they eat, and how much exercise they get, omitting the medical issues like metabolism. What they eat is controlled pretty much by parents and schools with lunch programs. Ditto on how much they eat. And exercise, to a great extent, is simply getting the kid up and moving.

Kids are concerned about how they look. I know of a third grader who wants to play sports, but he is heavy. He went to his uncle, who happens to be a coach, and asked for help. They do care.

So what contributes to the problem? I contend it's marketers, parents, society's idea of cool, and schools. Let's look at each, and then I have some solutions.

Marketers: Some alleged numbers: On Saturday morning TV, kids see seven ads per hour touting high fat and sugar. According to recent stats, we're spending $15 billion annually on kid advertising. Kids see as many as 100 messages a day. The charge is that we are creating an army of sugar-high automatons.

Parents: Parents should totally control their kids. Yeah, right. Research says that seven-year-olds and younger accept what we say in advertising as the truth. Heck, three-year-olds can identify brands using just their corporate logos. According to a survey commissioned by the Center for a New American Dream back in 2002, the average kid asks his parent for something nine times before the parent gives in. Ten percent of 12- and 13-year-olds ask for something more than 50 times before the parent gives in. And 55 percent of kids say their parents just cave. What's a mother to do under this assault?

Society and Schools Play a Role

Society: We want our kids to be experts in tennis, martial arts, dance, violin, chess, soccer, and wine. So, we set up a schedule for after school and Saturday that not only is it exhausting to the kid, but the parent, too. It's all in the name of broadening their horizons. I broadened my horizons as a kid by finding out what library paste tasted like and contemplating the iron pole and its relationship to my tongue on a cold day.

Schools: They feed kids five times a week, right? Only 6 percent of school lunch programs meet the United States Department of Agriculture guidelines. The schools respond that they can feed them anything, but if they won't eat it, what's the point?

So, Roy's thoughts on solutions: Let's stick to moderation, control, and education.

Moderation is the backbone of a famous weight-control program. You can eat anything as long as you don't eat too much or too often—you don't have to deny yourself anything. So it can be for kids.

I, for one, am tired of being blamed for kid obesity because of my marketing tactics.

I'm afraid control is a parental issue, with a little help from the schools. But come on guys, let's give parents a little help. Let's write a "Just Say No" program for parents teaching them how to say "no" without inflicting traumatic scars or losing the love of their offspring. I love the family dinner idea, so why not have it in the restaurant? How about a healthy kids' meal that you get a special prize for ordering, and once per week it's a hamburger and fries? How about only allowing advertising of healthy food in kids' programming?

What Marketers Can Do

Or let's do a marketing program as an industry that makes healthy foods cool to eat. I'm going to say it anyway: Let's be truthful in our advertising to kids about product merits. And, how about a quick-serve-sponsored exercise and outdoors program executed by the schools?

I, for one, am tired of being blamed for kid obesity because of my marketing tactics. Again, if we don't do something, here come the feds. More guidelines and bans of fast food from advertising in kids' programming, even though it has been shown in a couple of countries that doing so does not decrease the level of obesity. I would love to see an industry-funded committee of parents, kids, marketers, and educators attack the problem with no government intervention. What can we do to prevent kid obesity? And you can't say anything negative. Let the participants determine their own fate.

6

Fast Food Marketing Should Not Target Children

Jennifer L. Harris et al.

The following viewpoint was written by Jennifer L. Harris and eight other authors, all of whom are affiliated with the Rudd Center for Food Policy and Obesity at Yale University, a nonprofit research and public policy organization devoted to improving the world's diet, preventing obesity, and reducing weight stigma. Harris is the director of marketing initiatives at the Center.

Since the issue was first studied in 2010, there has not been much improvement in the nutritional quality of food offered at fast food restaurants or in the marketing of fast food to children and teens. Although some restaurants have started offering healthier options, overall the industry continues to promote food that is high in fat, calories, sugar, and sodium. In 2012, fast food restaurants spent $4.6 billion on advertising such unhealthy foods, much of it targeting children and teens. Fast food restaurants should do more to improve the nutritional quality of their food and stop targeting children and teens with marketing that encourages frequent restaurant visits and poor diet choices.

In 2010, researchers at the Yale Rudd Center for Food Policy & Obesity issued Fast Food FACTS. The report examined the nutritional quality of fast food menus, advertising on TV and the internet, and marketing practices inside restaurants. Three years later—using the same methods as the original Fast Food FACTS—this report quantifies changes in nutrition and marketing of fast food to children and teens.

The findings in the 2010 Fast Food FACTS report raised significant concerns about the effects of fast food marketing on the health of young people. Although all restaurants studied did offer some nutritious options, most fast food menu items—including kids' meal items—contained more calories, saturated fat, sugar, and/or sodium than recommended. The industry spent $4.2 billion on advertising to encourage frequent visits to fast food restaurants, targeting children as young as two years old. From 2003 to 2009, fast food TV advertising to children and teens increased by more than one-third, and the majority of fast food ads viewed by youth promoted restaurants' high-calorie, nutritionally poor regular menu items.

Objective and transparent data are necessary to evaluate restaurants' progress in reducing marketing that promotes consumption of unhealthy fast food by children and teens.

Since 2010, restaurants have implemented improvements. McDonald's and Chick-fil-A introduced healthier kids' meal options. Burger King and Sonic were among the first restaurants to join the National Restaurant Association's Kids LiveWell program and promised to offer at least one healthy meal and individual item for children. Restaurants also introduced healthier items to their regular menus, such as Burger King's grilled chicken wraps and fruit smoothies and Wendy's salads. At the same time, restaurants also introduced unhealthy items. For example, Taco Bell rolled out Doritos Locos Tacos, and Burger King introduced its Bacon Sundae. Both were supported by sophisticated marketing campaigns appealing to youth audiences.

Marketing to Children and Teens

Research published since 2010 also documents the need for continued concern about potential negative effects of fast food marketing on the diets of children and teens. More than one-third of youth consumed fast food on the previous day, including 33% of children (ages 2–11) and 41% of teens (ages 12–19). By comparison, 36% of adults consumed fast food on the previous day. When visiting fast food restaurants, the majority of children and teens order regular menu items, combo meals, and/or value menu items. At burger restaurants, only 44% of children under 6 and 31% of children ages 6 to 12 receive a kids' meal. In addition, since 2007 visits to fast food restaurants that included a kids' meal purchase have declined, with a 5% drop from 2010 to 2011. Further, one-quarter of teen visits to fast food restaurants were for an afternoon snack, a higher proportion of visits compared with all other age groups. Finally, consuming fast food increases daily calorie intake by 126 calories for children and 310 calories for teens, as well as consumption of sugary drinks, total sugar, saturated fat, and sodium.

Objective and transparent data are necessary to evaluate restaurants' progress in reducing marketing that promotes consumption of unhealthy fast food by children and teens.

Methods of Inquiry

Whenever possible, we used the same methods as the first Fast Food FACTS report to evaluate changes over time. The marketing analyses in this report focus on 18 restaurants: the 12 restaurants highlighted in the 2010 report plus six additional restaurants that ranked among the top-15 fast food restaurants in U.S. sales and/or had child-targeted messages on their websites and national TV advertising in 2012. The nutrition analyses exclude the pizza and coffee restaurants and focus on 12 restaurants. Time frames for the marketing analyses vary, but most analyses evaluate data through 2012. Nutrition data were collected in February 2013. It should be noted that fast food menus and marketing practices change continuously. The information presented in this report does not include new products or product reformulations, advertising campaigns, website redesigns, or other marketing programs introduced after July 2013.

Nearly all items on fast food menus—including kids' meal items—exceed recommended levels of calories, saturated fat, sodium, and/or sugar for children and teens.

Researchers collected menu item nutrient data from restaurant websites, supplemented by visits to fast food restaurants and calls to consumer helplines. We evaluate the nutritional quality of kids' meals and individual menu items on restaurant menus according to several criteria. The Nutrition Profiling Index (NPI) score provides a measure of the overall nutritional composition of individual menu items. The NPI score is based on the nutrition rating system established by Rayner and colleagues for the Food Standards Agency in the United Kingdom. To identify reasonable portion sizes for children and adolescents, we also compare total calories and total sodium for kids' meals and regular menu items against standards established by the Institute of Medicine's (IOM) School Meal guidelines for preschoolers, elementary school-age children, and teenagers. Lastly, we evaluate menu items according to other established criteria for nutrition quality, including the Children's Food and Beverage Advertising Initiative's (CFBAI) new uniform category-specific nutrition criteria for meals that can be advertised in child-directed media and the National Restaurant Association's Kids LiveWell nutrition standards for healthy children's meals.

The marketing analyses document advertising spending and marketing on TV and in digital media (restaurant websites, display advertising on third-party websites, social media, and mobile devices). We also identify marketing that appears to be targeted to children, teens, and black and Hispanic youth. Sources of marketing data include media exposure and spending data purchased from Nielsen and comScore, content analyses of advertisements on children's TV, and additional analyses using information collected from company websites and monitoring of business and consumer press.

Nutrition Results

Kids' meal options have improved since 2010. Most restaurants offer more healthy sides and beverages and some also offer healthy main dishes for their kids' meals. Restaurants also added a few new healthy options to their regular menus. However, nearly all items on fast food menus—including kids' meal items—exceed recommended levels of calories, saturated fat, sodium, and/or sugar for children and teens.

From 2010 to 2013, the nutritional quality of individual items offered with kids' meals improved at some restaurants. All restaurants except Taco Bell offered at least one healthy side option for their kids' meals; three-quarters of restaurants with kids' meals increased healthy beverage options; and McDonald's introduced half-portions of french fries and apples as the default sides in Happy Meals. There was also a 54% increase in the number of different kids' meals available, consisting of a kids' main dish, side, and beverage. In total, the 12 restaurants examined in 2013 with special kids' menus offered 5,427 possible kids' meal combinations.

However, there was no change in the percent of kids' meal combinations that qualified as healthy meals for children. As in 2010, less than 1% of all kids' meal combinations met recommended nutrition standards: just 33 possible kids' meals met all nutrition criteria for elementary school-age children and 15 met standards for preschoolers. Kids' meal main dishes were especially problematic. Only five restaurants (Subway, Burger King, Taco Bell, Arby's, and Jack in the Box) offered even one kids' meal main dish option that was not too high in saturated fat and/or sodium. Further, just 3% of kids' meal combinations met the industry's own revised CFBAI nutrition standards or Kids LiveWell standards.

On average, U.S. preschoolers viewed 2.8 fast food ads on TV every day in 2012, children (6–11 years) viewed 3.2 ads per day, and teens viewed 4.8 ads per day.

Number of Menu Items Jumps

On regular menus, there was also a dramatic increase in the number of menu items offered by fast food restaurants, but the proportion of healthy versus unhealthy menu items remained the same. From 2010 to 2013, McDonald's, Subway, Burger King, and Taco Bell averaged 71 additional menu items per restaurant (+35%), and the number of snack and dessert items offered increased 88%. McDonald's continued to have the highest proportion of menu items that met nutrition criteria for teens (24%). At Burger King, Subway, and Wendy's, no more than 20% of items qualified as nutritious. McDonald's, Subway, Taco Bell, and Sonic did advertise healthy menus consisting of items they designated as healthier or lower-calorie. However, less than half of healthy menu items at McDonald's, Subway, and Sonic met all nutrition criteria. Healthy menus from Subway and Sonic were less likely to meet nutrition criteria in 2013 than in 2010. In addition, all restaurants continued to offer large or extra-large soft drinks with 350 to 850 calories per serving and burger restaurants offered large french fries with 470 to 610 calories.

In 2012, fast food restaurants spent $4.6 billion in total on all advertising, an 8% increase over 2009. For context, the biggest advertiser, McDonald's, spent 2.7 times as much to advertise its products ($972 million) as all fruit, vegetable, bottled water, and milk advertisers combined ($367 million).

On average, U.S. preschoolers viewed 2.8 fast food ads on TV every day in 2012, children (6–11 years) viewed 3.2 ads per day, and teens viewed 4.8 ads per day. Six companies were responsible for more than 70% of all TV ads viewed by children and teens; McDonald's, Subway, Burger King, Domino's, Yum! Brands (Taco Bell, Pizza Hut, KFC), and Wendy's.

Marketing to Children

There were a few positive developments in fast food marketing to children. From 2009 to 2012, total fast food TV advertising seen by children ages 6 to 11 declined by 10%. McDonald's and Burger King (the two biggest advertisers in 2009) reduced their advertising to children by 13% and 50%, respectively. Marketing to children on the internet also declined. Three popular child-targeted websites (Dairy Queen's DeeQs.com, McDonald's LineRider.com, and Burger King's ClubBK.com) were discontinued, as was McDonald's site for preschoolers (Ronald.com). Just one site (HappyMeal.com) had more than 100,000 monthly unique child visitors in 2012, compared with four sites in 2009.

However, there are many reasons for continued concern. Despite the decline in TV advertising to 6- to 11-year-olds, advertising to very young children (ages 2–5) did not change from 2009 to 2012, and the majority of fast food restaurants stepped up their TV advertising to children. Among the top-25 advertisers, 19 increased advertising to preschoolers, and 14 increased ads to older children. Of note, Domino's and Wendy's increased advertising to children by 44% and 13%, respectively, which were approximately six times their rates of increase in advertising to teens. Further, McDonald's continued to advertise more to children than to teens or adults on TV—the only restaurant to do so. On the internet, McDonald's also placed 34 million display ads for Happy Meals per month—up 63% from 2009. Three-quarters of Happy Meal ads appeared on kids' websites, such as Nick.com, Roblox

.com, and CartoonNetwork.com. In addition, child-targeted advergames (i.e., branded games) have gone mobile with McDonald's "McPlay" and Wendy's "Pet Play Games" mobile apps.

Several restaurants continued to target teens directly with marketing for unhealthy products.

A few restaurants did advertise their healthier kids' meals, but kids' meals represented only one-quarter of fast food ads viewed by children on TV. McDonald's Happy Meals were the most frequently advertised products to children, followed by Domino's pizza, Subway sandwiches, Wendy's lunch/dinner items, and Pizza Hut pizza. Burger King and Subway kids' meals ranked 16 and 19, respectively. In apparent contradiction of Children's Advertising Review Unit (CARU) guidelines that advertising to children must focus primarily on the product being sold (i.e., food), Subway placed ads with a primary focus on the brand (not the food) on children's networks, and Burger King placed ads that focused primarily on child-targeted promotions. In addition, Wendy's and Subway advertised regular menu items—including Frostys, Baconator burgers, and Footlong sandwiches—directly to children on children's networks, including Nickelodeon and Cartoon Network. McDonald's advertised its Filet-o-fish sandwich and other regular menu items on kids' websites, including Nick .com and CartoonNetwork.com.

Marketing to Teens

There were fewer positive trends in fast food marketing to teens. The overall nutritional quality of fast food products advertised to teens on TV did improve. Although the average number of fast food TV ads viewed by teens did not change from 2009 to 2012, average calories in TV ads viewed declined 16%, and the proportion of calories from sugar and saturated fat improved from 37% in 2010 to 28% in 2013. In addition, the number of display ads placed by fast food restaurants on youth websites declined by more than half, from 470 million ad views per month in 2009 to 210 million in 2012.

However, several restaurants continued to target teens directly with marketing for unhealthy products. Although teens watch 30% less TV than do adults, they saw as many or more TV advertisements for Taco Bell, Sonic, and Starbucks compared with adults. Thus these restaurants likely purchased advertising in media viewed by relatively more adolescents than adults. Burger King Smoothies were the only nutritious regular menu item among those advertised most frequently to teens. In addition, three restaurants substantially increased their display advertising on youth websites: KFC (+138%), Subway (+450%), and Starbucks (+330%). In contrast to the decline in child visits to restaurant websites, the number of teen visitors increased for more than half of the websites analyzed both in 2010 and 2013, including Subway.com (+102%), Starbucks.com (+92%), and McDonalds.com (+75%). Three fast food websites (PizzaHut.com, McDonalds.com, and Dominos.com) averaged 270,000 or more unique teen visitors per month.

Black children and teens saw approximately 60% more fast food ads than white youth, due largely to greater TV viewing.

Further, fast food marketing via mobile devices and social media—media that are popular with teens—grew exponentially in the three years examined. Fast food restaurants placed six billion display ads on Facebook in 2012, 19% of all their online display advertising. Dunkin' Donuts and Wendy's placed more than one-half of their online ads on Facebook. Starbucks was most popular on social media, with 35 million Facebook likes and 4.2 million Twitter followers, followed by

McDonald's and Subway, which each had 23+ million Facebook likes and 1.4+ million Twitter followers. From 2010 to 2013, increases in the number of Facebook likes and Twitter followers ranged from 200% to 6400%. Six fast food restaurants had more than 10 million likes on Facebook in 2013. Taco Bell's YouTube videos were viewed nearly 14 million times. In addition, ten restaurants offered branded smartphone apps with interactive features, including order functions and special offers. Papa John's and Pizza Hut mobile apps averaged 700,000+ unique visitors per month.

Targeted Marketing to Racial and Ethnic Minority Youth

Fast food restaurants also continued to target black and Hispanic youth, populations at high risk for obesity and related diseases. Increased advertising on Spanish-language TV raises special concerns. Combined advertising spending on Spanish-language TV by all fast food restaurants increased 8% from 2009 to 2012. KFC and Burger King increased their spending by 35% to 41% while reducing English-language advertising, and Domino's and Subway increased Spanish-language advertising by more than 15%. Hispanic preschoolers' exposure to fast food ads on Spanish-language TV increased by 16% reaching almost one ad viewed per day. They also saw 100 more of these ads than older Hispanic children or teens saw. However, just 5% of Spanish-language ads viewed by Hispanic children promoted kids' meals.

As in 2009, black children and teens saw approximately 60% more fast food ads than white youth, due largely to greater TV viewing. However, advertising for Starbucks, Popeyes, Papa John's, and some Burger King products appeared during programming watched relatively more often by black youth. Black and Hispanic youth were more likely than their white and non-Hispanic peers to visit one-third or more of all fast food websites. For instance, Hispanic youth were

30% more likely to visit HappyMeal.com, and black youth were 44% more likely to visit the site.

Recommendations for Restaurants

This report documents a few positive developments in the nutritional quality of fast food menu offerings and marketing to children. However, the pace of improvement is slow and unlikely to reduce young people's overconsumption of high-calorie, nutritionally poor fast food.

Fast food restaurants should stop targeting children and teens with marketing that encourages frequent visits to restaurants.

Fast food restaurants must do more to improve the overall nutritional quality of the products they sell.

- Participating restaurants are only required to apply CFBAI nutrition standards to kids' meals presented in their advertising, while Kids LiveWell restaurants must offer just one meal that meets program standards. Industry standards for healthy kids' meals should apply to the majority of kids' meal combinations available for purchase—not a mere 3%.

- Automatically providing healthier sides as the default option for kids' meals works. McDonald's switch to smaller portions of apples and french fries has increased the percent of children who receive fruit with their kids' meals: 28% in 2010 versus 86% in 2013. All fast food restaurants should make healthy sides and beverages the default in their kids' meals.

- Restaurants should increase the proportion of lower-calorie, healthier items on their menus and make them available at a reasonable price.

Fast food restaurants should stop targeting children and teens with marketing that encourages frequent visits to restaurants.

- Restaurants should stop advertising anything but the healthiest children's menu items on children's TV networks and third-party kids' websites.

- Restaurants should stop targeting children with marketing practices that take advantage of their developmental vulnerabilities or reach them behind parents' backs. These practices include TV ads that focus on branding or promotions instead of food, mobile advergame apps, and online advertising with links to kids' advergame sites.

- Preschoolers should not be exposed to daily ads for regular menu items—advertisers should revise their media plans to ensure that very young children are protected from these messages. In particular, advertisers on Spanish-language TV must do more to keep their unhealthy messages from these very young and vulnerable viewers.

- Restaurants should acknowledge that teens are also highly influenced by advertising and deserve protection from marketing for fast food products that can damage their health.

- Definitions of child-targeted marketing used in industry self-regulation should include children in middle school aged 12–14.

- Restaurants also should establish age limits on fast food marketing to youth via social media and mobile devices—venues that take advantage of teens' greater susceptibility to peer influence and impulsive actions.

To ensure the health of our children, restaurants must do much more to reduce young people's overconsumption of fast food that is high in calories, saturated fat, sodium, and sugar. If restaurants choose instead to make healthy menu items the norm, not the exception, and market them more effectively, fast food restaurants could attract lifelong customers who will also live longer, healthier lives.

7

Parents Are Responsible for What Children Eat, Not Restaurants

The kNOw Youth Media

The kNOw Youth Media in Fresno, California, is one of six youth media programs incubated under the umbrella of Pacific News Service/New America Media, a nonprofit alternative news service.

Childhood obesity is a serious issue, but fast food restaurants are unfairly blamed for the problem. The real responsibility lies with parents, whose job it is to keep their children safe and healthy. Parents need to set a good example about food and exercise in order to create healthy habits in their children, but the first step is that parents need to start thinking of obesity as a dangerous condition that can lead to serious health problems or even be life threatening. As parents come to understand that obesity can literally be a matter of life and death, they will have more incentive to take action and assert control over their children's behavior and unhealthy eating habits.

In a modern society, there are several difficulties. Along with the murders and diseases, obesity ranks as one of the chief problems in today's communities. Childhood obesity is very serious and it seems as if nobody wants to take responsibility for it. There has been plenty of controversy of who is to blame for the epidemic. Whether it is the government, fast-food restaurants, parents or even the children, none of these groups seem willing to account for the predicament. In a 2002 *Sacramento Bee* column, "The Battle against Fast Food Begins in the Home," Daniel Weintraub demands parents should be held accountable for their children's excess weight. Weintraub is correct. Parents should take responsibility for this growing epidemic.

A parent's job is to look after their kid and keep them from harm's way. How is it that parents can be liable for everything else regarding their children, yet not this? "We have laws against leaving a loaded weapon with our children, why should food be any different?" Weintraub asks. This lack of protective laws is changing, as some legislators are crafting laws to guard the health of children. SB 622, authored this February [2013] and currently moving through the Calif. legislature, would institute a state soda tax. The proceeds of this tax would support obesity prevention.

Childhood obesity is not just another issue, it is a life threatening issue.

Parents Know Fast Food Is Unhealthy

There are many excuses for who is to blame for children's obesity, and blame often is given to restaurants such as McDonald's. A general assumption concerning McDonald's or any fast food is that it is unhealthy to eat. Parents are not ignorant to that fact. Fast food meals consist of extra sugar, grease and calories. Why do parents continue to feed their children fast food if it is not good for them? Parents, knowingly or unknowingly, are basically giving their children that loaded gun. Just as much as the gun is dangerous, so is fast food. They both can potentially be deadly.

People in general do not see obesity in children as the urgent, life-threatening problem that it is. Parents might pay more attention to having a "fat" kid than raising a child struggling with obesity. Don't get me wrong, "obese" and "fat" may seem like similar words, but they have their differences. Being classified as "fat" can be based on your appearance, however, getting identified as "obese" means that medically speaking it is critical for your well-being to change your diet. That doesn't mean eat less, but change what you eat and how much you move throughout the day.

Health Versus Appearance

Parents might just assume that they don't want their children to eat certain things because they're afraid they could become fat. Some parents might even tell their child, "No candy until after dinner!" However, limiting some foods never really works. My mother is like that. My younger brother is a big boy. He is always eating too. He doesn't just snack though, he eats healthy meals as well. My mom will always scold him, "No Nathan, you already ate!," then later she will give in. She is not worried about whether or not the type of food is healthy for his body or if he exercises enough, all she cares about is making sure her son doesn't stay big. It should not be this way. Parents shouldn't just be worried about the kid gaining weight or their appearance, but worry about what a poor diet can do to a child's body. Obesity is a big deal for any age, but when it attacks a child it can cause many problems.

Childhood obesity is not just another issue, it is a life threatening issue. It is a caloric imbalance. The children's unhealthy eating habits can lead to many consequences. One of the main effects of childhood obesity is cardiovascular disease. More than 70 percent of children suffering with obesity end up with cardiovascular disease. Other outcomes are high cholesterol and high blood pressure. Children as early as 5 years old suffering with obesity can get pre-diabetes. Pre-diabetes can result in bone and joint problems.

Not only is this problem dangerous, but without the support from parents it can increase. In the past 30 years this disease has nearly tripled. In 2008, more than one third of children were overweight and obese. The rate of childhood obesity jumped from 7 percent to 20 percent.

Watching eating habits of children is easier said than done. For instance, Weintraub states, "It is not easy, especially when both parents are working or there is only one parent in the home. Fast food is fast. It can also seem cheap; at least before you start adding the fries and sodas and desserts." In other words, Weintraub simply understands that taking on the task of a parent alone can be a struggle, without watching your child's weight. However sooner [or] later, it has to be realized that it is the parents' responsibility.

Some Families Have Limited Options

This does not go to show that parents are bad people who deliberately choose for their children to be fat. After realizing the consequences of childhood obesity, some people might claim that parents who don't control what their children eat are participating in child abuse. However that is not the case. Some parents don't have options for healthy choices. There are many families out there without the proper resources to exercise with their families or provide a better diet.

Parents play a huge influence in their child's life. Parents can encourage healthy lifestyle habits.

In the article, "The Health Toll of Immigration," Sabrina Tavernise identifies immigrants as the group who struggles most with this problem.

Immigrants came to this country in hope to find better opportunities. They eventually had children. When they made enough money they would go out to eat. As immigrants in America with more food options than ever before, eating out with their families proved their economic status. With the low prices of fast food, immigrants were able to enjoy the luxury of eating out, but this luxury eventually turned into a necessity. The American-born children of immigrants were forced to eat out [rather] than a dinner at home because of the lack of money. They would not go out to exercise because of the fear of getting caught by immigration officers. As a result the American-born children of immigrants suffered more than the parents did. So the question then becomes how can we help the parents stop childhood obesity?

What Can Parents Do?

With the appropriate actions there are ways to limit and even prevent childhood obesity. Parents play a huge influence in their child's life. Parents can encourage healthy lifestyle habits. They can also use schools for support to raise awareness about the growing epidemic and its factors. Because obesity is partly based on behaviors, exercising and eating healthier meals as a family would help limit the chances of becoming overweight. They can exercise at home and even find cheaper recipes that are a healthy choice. Parents can especially benefit from any of these vigorous choices. It can help lower their children's risk of developing obesity along with any other related diseases.

The essence of Weintraub's argument is that presenting children with the appropriate eating and behavioral habits relies solely on the parents. Parents are given the role to protect their offspring. Parents have some control over their children's decisions in life regarding everything else. It is time that the parents are given not just responsibility for childhood obesity, but the information and tools they need to help prevent it. Childhood obesity is not based on the government, or any fast food restaurant. Childhood obesity stops with the group of people who are trusted to raise them, the parents—and they need all the help they can get.

Requiring Calories on Fast Food Menus Promotes Better Choices

Susan Craig and Chanel Caraway

Susan Craig and Chanel Caraway work in the press office of the New York City Department of Health and Mental Hygiene.

One year after New York City enacted a law requiring calorie counts on restaurant menus, there is evidence that the practice helps consumers eat fewer calories and make healthier food choices. One in six consumers interviewed for the study said they used the calorie information on menus to make food purchases. Consumers at fast food chains in particular reduced their caloric intake as a result of the menu labeling. The New York study is the most extensive assessment of menu labeling to date, and city officials are hopeful that the practice will create a long-term public health benefit.

Editor's Note: As part of the federal government's health care reform, the Affordable Care Act of 2010 mandates restaurants that have twenty outlets or more to provide calorie counts for the food items on their menus. The US Food and Drug Administration (FDA) is the agency responsible for establishing the guidelines for such notices, but the FDA had not set any final rules as of mid-August 2014. The restaurant industry has fought the mandate, and pizza chains and movie theaters are reportedly seeking an exemption.

New Yorkers who bought lunch at several major fast food chains used posted menu calorie counts to make lower calorie choices, according to a study released today in the *British Medical Journal*. Researchers surveyed a sample of New Yorkers before and after the March 2008 regulation for fast food chains to post calories went into effect. In spring 2009, one year after the trend-setting New York City law became effective, one out of every six fast food customers surveyed said they used posted calorie information to make food buying decisions and these customers purchased 106 fewer calories than those who did not see or use the calorie information. The NYC law for calorie posting was adopted nationally through the health care reform bill in 2010 and will go into effect nation-wide within the next year. This is the most extensive study of the effect of menu labeling to date.

One in six customers (15%) reported using the calorie information to make their purchase, and the customers purchased an average of 106 fewer calories.

"New Yorkers who want to limit their calories are using posted calorie information to do so," said Thomas Farley, New York City Health Commissioner. "By requiring fast food chains to post the amount of calories in food items, we've made it easier for New Yorkers to make more informed choices about the food they eat. This customer survey shows that people who are taking calorie counts into account when they order are purchasing fewer calories as a result. Posted calorie listings help consumers make healthier choices. Considering the extremely high rates of obesity, these types of systematic changes to the food environment are needed to make a difference in combating today's obesity epidemic."

Obesity in New York

Calorie posting and other food improvement efforts are aimed at tackling obesity rates in New York City, which are at an all-time high in both adults and children. Currently nearly six in ten New York City adults are overweight or obese. The leading causes of death in New York City and across the nation are associated with obesity, including cardiovascular disease, cancer and diabetes. Consuming a healthy diet—one that is high in fruits and vegetables, low in fat and that meets daily calorie recommendations—is [one] of the most important factors that can protect against these chronic diseases.

To assess whether the City's innovative calorie labeling policy would result in any change in calories purchased, researchers surveyed more than 15,000 lunchtime customers and reviewed their register receipts from 168 locations of the top 11 fast food chains in New York City in 2007 and 2009, before and after the law went into effect.

One in six customers (15%) reported using the calorie information to make their purchase, and the customers purchased an average of 106 fewer calories. The researchers also determined that customers at three of the major fast food chains significantly reduced the calorie content of the food items they purchased in 2009 as compared with purchases in 2007. Lunchgoers at Au Bon Pain purchased 80 fewer calories. KFC customers purchased 59 fewer calories after calorie labeling went into effect and McDonald's patrons purchased 44 fewer calories according to receipts. Together, these three chains represented 42% of all customers in the study.

Subway Skews the Data

One chain, Subway, showed a significant increase in calories purchased post regulation. However, the sandwich maker ran a $5 foot-long sub sandwich promotion during the survey period, resulting in a tripling of the percentage of customers who purchased the 12-inch sandwich. In 2007 (before regulation), one in four customers purchased a 12 inch sub; in 2009 (post regulation and during the $5 promotion) three in four customers purchased the 12-inch sandwich. Data did not show a statistically significant change in calories purchased overall at all food chains.

"As calorie labeling spreads nationwide and internationally, more consumers will be able to easily access calorie information and restaurant chains will have a greater incentive to reformulate their products and offer healthier options," said Dr. Lynn Silver, a co-author of the BMJ paper and director of the Office of Science and Policy in the Health Department's Division of Health Promotion and Disease Prevention. "More complete evaluation of the long-term effects of the policy will be possible over time, but these initial findings in New York City are encouraging. For customers who don't examine calorie information, increasing the proportion of lower calorie offerings is important. While calorie labeling alone will not solve the obesity epidemic, it is an important tool to inform the public and provide an incentive for the restaurant industry to improve its offerings."

Consumers Underestimate Calories

Today, across the nation almost 50% of the food dollar is spent outside the home. A link between fast food consumption and excessive calorie intake has been documented by several research studies. Studies show that customers often underestimate the number of calories in restaurant meals. Before 2008, nutrition information for fast food items was seldom available at the point of purchase, when consumers can use it to make buying decisions. The Health Department passed the 2008 regulation to post calorie information at the point of purchase in order to give New Yorkers an opportunity to make more informed food choices.

9

Requiring Calories on Fast Food Menus Makes No Difference

Anne Hart

Anne Hart is a freelance writer who specializes in nutrition and health journalism, science writing, and culture in the media.

Customers usually ignore or fail to see calorie postings at fast food restaurants, but even if they do, the information doesn't influence their food purchasing decisions or reduce the number of calories they eat, a recent study in Philadelphia has found. Researchers also say the presence of menu labeling does not change the frequency with which consumers visit fast food chain restaurants in the future. The Affordable Care Act of 2010 requires restaurants that have twenty outlets or more nationwide to provide calorie counts for the food and drink items on their menus, but making such postings mandatory makes no difference in consumer behavior.

Mandatory calorie postings at fast-food chains often are ignored or unseen, but the postings don't influence food choice, says a new study. Population health expert Brian Elbel of the NYU [New York University] Langone Medical Center/[NYU] School of Medicine presented findings on November 15, 2013 at a leading scientific conference on obesity, the Obesity Society's annual scientific meeting, held this week in Atlanta, Georgia.

Posting the calorie content of menu items at major fast-food chains in Philadelphia, per federal law, does not change purchasing habits or decrease the number of calories that those customers consume. The results echo those conducted by the same researchers among low-income neighborhoods in New York City before and after calorie-labels were mandated there in July 2008, according to the November 15, 2013 news release, "Mandatory calorie postings at fast-food chains often ignored or unseen, does not influence food choice."

Obesity Week 2013 is the inaugural event co-locating the American Society of Metabolic and Bariatric Surgery (ASMBS) and The Obesity Society (TOS) annual meetings. In doing so, the more than 60 years of combined experience in the study of obesity and its management are reflected in an interdisciplinary program from which all attendees will benefit.

There is limited scientific evidence from real-world studies to support calorie labeling.

Consumers Don't Notice Calorie Labeling

"What we're seeing is that many consumers, particularly vulnerable groups, do not report noticing calorie labeling information and even fewer report using labeling to purchase fewer calories," says lead study author Dr. Brian Elbel, in the news release. Elbel is the assistant professor of Population Health and Health Policy at NYU School of Medicine. "After labeling began in Philadelphia, about 10 percent of the respondents in our study said that calorie labels at fast-food chains resulted in them choosing fewer calories."

As part of an effort to encourage people to make healthier food choices, the Patient Protection and Affordable Care Act mandates that restaurant chains with 20 or more locations nationally must post the calorie content of all regular food and drink items on their menu board or printed menus.

Different Groups Respond Differently

Yet there is limited scientific evidence from real-world studies to support calorie labeling. Moreover, little is understood about how calorie labels will impact different populations. Obesity affects more than one third of Americans, but hits low-income, urban neighborhoods hardest. "Studies have not generally examined whether labeling is more or less effective for particular subgroups," says Dr. Elbel in the news release.

Dr. Elbel and team set out to assess the impact of calorie labels at fast-food chains in the wake of the new legislation. In their latest study, conducted in Philadelphia, researchers collected receipts from more than 2,000 customers, ages 18 to 64, who visited McDonald's and Burger King restaurants during lunch or dinner before and after February 2010, when the calorie-label law went into effect in Philadelphia.

Each customer was asked a short series of questions, including how often they had visited "big chain" fast food restaurants in the last week; whether they noticed calorie information in the restaurant; and if so, whether they used the information to purchase more or less food than they otherwise would have at the restaurant.

The research team also commissioned a professional survey firm to simultaneously conduct a random phone survey of residents within the city limits of Philadelphia. Respondents aged 18 to 64 were asked a series of questions, including whether they had consumed any "big chain" fast food within the last three months. If they had, they were asked a series of additional questions about how often they eat fast food, along with demographic questions and their height and weight.

Who Noticed What

Researchers found that only 34 percent of McDonald's customers noticed the labels posted to menu boards, compared to 49 percent of Burger King customers.

Respondents with less education (high school or lower) were less likely to notice the labels. Moreover, respondents reported eating fast food more than 5 times a week, both before and after the labels were posted. There was no decrease in visiting fast food restaurants reported after calorie labeling began in Philadelphia.

(As a control, the researchers also surveyed customers of both chains in Baltimore, where calorie-labels are not mandated. About 70% of the customers surveyed in both cities were African American.) "We found no difference in calories purchased or fast-food visits after the introduction of the policy," says Dr. Elbel, according to the news release. "Given the limits of labeling reported here and in other studies, it's clear that just posting calories is often not enough to change behavior among all populations. We need to consider other, more robust interventional policies in places where obesity is most prevalent."

10

Fast Food Workers Are Exploited and Underpaid

John Logan

John Logan is professor and director of labor and employment studies at San Francisco State University.

Because workers in the fast food industry are poorly paid and typically denied full-time hours and the benefits that come with them, they are twice as likely as workers in other industries to rely on public assistance programs to make ends meet. The meager incomes of fast food workers are often further reduced through wage theft, unpaid overtime, and other dubious business practices, effectively trapping workers in dead-end jobs and promoting a cycle of poverty. Fast food workers deserve higher wages, better benefits, and more full-time shifts, which is what workers have been calling for in strikes nationwide since November 2012.

Fast food workers engaged yesterday [December 5, 2013] in one-day walkouts in one hundred cities, and almost a hundred other cities saw protests against poverty-level wages. A broad alliance of community, civil rights, religious and student organizations supported the actions.

One-day walkouts by fast food workers started in New York City in November 2012—the industry's first ever strikes—and have spread like wildfire since then. By August the strikes had extended to sixty cities around the country, including the South and West Coast, and today's actions will encompass such unlikely locations as Charleston, South Carolina. The protests have grown quickly because the message that poverty-level wages and poor working conditions are indefensible has resonated so strongly with the industry's workers. Faced with rock-bottom wages and benefits, and little opportunity for career advancement, fast food workers have few other options when it comes to improving their situation.

The protests have highlighted the urgent need for higher wages, better benefits and more full-time jobs. Fast food jobs fail to offer workers a route out of poverty. Workers earn a median wage of $8.69 per hour, 83 percent earn less than $10.10 per hour, and opportunities for advancement are extremely limited. Low paid front-line occupations comprise over 89 percent of all jobs in the industry, while franchise owners make up just 1 percent of all positions. A majority of fast food workers, who are significantly older and better educated than industry representatives make out, are denied full-time work. But the industry's wages are so low that even those front-line employees who work 40 hours per week are often forced to rely on public assistance, and only 13 percent have access to employer-sponsored healthcare programs.

Don't be misled by the disingenuous arguments of hugely profitable corporations that pay poverty wages and rely on enormous public subsidies.

Poor Pay Pushes People onto Welfare

Most fast food workers have experienced "wage theft"—such as failure to pay overtime or receive required rest breaks, improper deductions from paychecks, out-of-pocket deductions for register stoppages, and late or bounced paychecks—including 84 percent of workers in New York City. But it does [not] need to be this way. In addition to benefitting workers, the fast food industry itself would likely benefit from higher wages, as this would reduce extremely high rates of employee turn-over and result in productivity and efficiency gains.

But it is not only fast food workers that suffer from the industry's business model. Every year, taxpayers subsidize fast-food corporations to the tune of almost $7 billion per year, and fast food workers are more than twice as likely to receive public assistance than are other workers. Fast food workers and their dependents are among the nation's biggest users of Medicaid, Children's Health Insurance Program, Earned Income Tax Credit, Supplemental Nutrition Assistance Program, and Temporary Assistance for Needy Families. McDonald's—the nation's largest fast food employer of workers who depend on public assistance—has an advice line that encourages its underpaid employees to seek food stamps and Medicaid. When McDonald's, Pizza Hut, KFC, Burger King, and Taco Bell—all highly-profitably operations—refuse to pay their front-line employees a living wage, it's not just fast food workers who pay the price. U.S. taxpayers end up picking up the tab.

Republican Party Fights Wage Increase

How has the GOP [Republican Party] reacted to the morally indefensible issue of poverty-level wages? Instead of standing up for better wages and working conditions, it has attacked the groups supporting the rights of low-wage workers. Instead of standing up against the enormous public subsidy of billion dollar corporations, it has stood against tax payers and with employers that advise workers to seek Medicare and food stamps. It is little wonder, then, that the fast food industry costs the public $3.5 billion per year in Medicare and food stamps subsidies alone. The only policy solutions offered by the GOP would mean more misery for fast food workers and greater financial hardship for middle-class Americans.

Don't be misled by the disingenuous arguments of hugely profitable corporations that pay poverty wages and rely on enormous public subsidies. The message of the strikes and protests is indisputable: fast food workers need a raise and a voice.

11

In Defense of the
Fast Food Industry

Jason Leavitt

Jason Leavitt is the founder of LeavittBrothers.com, an advisory service for stock traders.

Workers in the fast food industry bemoan their low pay and lack of benefits, but there is simply no room to expand wages because the individual owners of chain restaurant franchises would no longer be able to make a profit from their business. If the government forces a significant wage increase, the cost would be passed on to consumers. The fast food industry currently provides millions of jobs for individuals who have limited skills and training, but those workers could eventually be replaced by automation in order to keep costs down. Fast food workers are paid according to their minimal skill level and it is better to have a low-paying job than no job at all.

Fast food workers want higher wages. They typically make $7.50–$10.00 an hour, but they want more. They want $15.00 an hour, enough to live comfortably on.

They have their sympathizers; they also have those who will stand and laugh at their demands. From the stance of the latter camp, this write-up is in support of the industry which provides millions of jobs, albeit low-paying ones.

Sympathizers think McDonald's and others should voluntarily pay higher wages, swallow the cost and make less profit.

This sounds nice, as if McDonald's is serving the greater good in society by acting as a pseudo government. But those who believe this don't understand how the fast food industry works, or at least how the franchise industry works.

Higher Wages Are Not Realistic

The real reason wages can't go up is because they can't. What fast food employees and their supporters don't realize is there's a big difference between McDonald's, which is a massive publicly traded company that spans the globe, and an individual McDonald's restaurant, which is independently owned by a single person or a small group of people.

In an industry that must run a tight ship and be extremely efficient there is no room on the balance sheets of individual stores to suddenly raise wages.

McDonald's Corporation charges its franchisees four percent of sales and an additional fee which could be as much as 8.5 percent. This comes off the top, not after all other expenses are paid. So if McDonald's wages were to double, the franchisees would be responsible for the entire cost, not McDonald's Corporation.

Individual restaurants simply aren't that profitable to be able to swallow such an increase. McDonald's loves the dollar menu, but truth be told, individual franchisee hate it because margins are paper thin. If you double wages, a franchisee literally would lose money every time an item off the dollar menu was purchased.

In an industry that must run a tight ship and be extremely efficient there is no room on the balance sheets of individual stores to suddenly raise wages. It's flat-out impossible.

The Consequences

But let's say they do. Let's say Congress mandates $15.00 an hour to all fast food employees. Here's what will happen.

First, prices will need to be raised to cover the expense. This will cause sales to drop for two reasons:

1. The higher cost will simply turn some customers away. After all, they eat fast food because it's fast and cheap. If it's no longer cheap, there's no incentive to eat there.

2. Higher prices would mean you're selling a low quality item for a medium price. This would cause many customers to seek out a medium quality product at the same medium price. Why spend six bucks for a Big Mac when you can get a very good 1/2-pound burger at Fuddruckers (are they still in business?) for the same price?

Next, the fast food industry will invest heavily in automation. Look no further than Europe, where wages are much higher than the US, to see where we'd head. [There's a] CNET article from two years ago that talks about 7,000 touch-screen cashiers being added to McDonald's restaurants. Hey McDonald's employees, don't you think it's better to have a low-paying job than no job at all? Because if you want more money, you will be replaced.

Hey fast food employees, it's better to have a relatively low-paying job than no job at all.

Think you're safe because you cook the burgers instead of taking orders? Think again. Taking it a step further, the cooking process will be automated. Go to YouTube and do a search for almost anything that is built: "how drywall is made" for example. You'll quickly realize almost everything that takes place in the "back of the house" in a fast food restaurant can be automated.

An article on GIZMODO from last year talks about a company in San Francisco that has developed a machine that can pump out 360 made-to-order burgers an hour, and get this, the machine only takes up 24 square feet.

If wages are raised to $15.00 an hour, fast food restaurants of the future will resemble today's gas stations—only one or two employees and lots of automation. Restaurants will become big vending machines. Place your order (and pay for it), wait a minute and here it comes down the conveyor belt. Perhaps there'll be a person that smiles and tells you to have a great day when you pick it up.

These changes will most definitely happen slowly if wages go up much, so the current workers are probably somewhat safe. It's the 10 year-olds that are coming up behind that will be screwed. But there is one immediate effect (other than sales declining and therefore layoffs). Jobs will go to more experienced, higher skilled workers.

At $15 an hour, school teachers who only make $30K per year will look to pick up a part-time side job to make a few bucks. If you're a McDonald's franchisee, who would you hire? A responsible, part-time school teacher or the unknown, possibly irresponsible and unmotivated high school kid? The answer is obvious. If teens have to compete with more experienced adults for the same jobs, they'll lose every time.

Hey fast food employees, it's better to have a relatively low-paying job than no job at all. Be careful what you wish for.

Couple side notes. . . .

I know not all fast food restaurants are primarily franchisee-owned. Chipotle, for example, is entirely corporate owned, so any increase in wages would go directly to the parent company.

12

Fast Food Is Physically Addictive

The Scripps Research Institute

Based in California, The Scripps Research Institute is one of the world's largest independent, nonprofit biomedical research organizations.

Researchers believe that the same brain mechanisms that cause people to become addicted to drugs like cocaine or heroin are responsible for the compulsion many people feel to binge on high-calorie, high-fat foods. Scientists believe that junk food overstimulates pleasure reward circuits in the brain, much as other addictive substances do. Lab experiments showed that rats would rather receive an electric shock than miss a meal of junk food. The rats that became "junk food junkies" began to persistently overeat, grew obese, and developed health problems. The study is strong evidence that the tendency to overeat certain foods is driven by a physical addiction in the same way that drug use is.

In a newly published study, scientists from The Scripps Research Institute have shown for the first time that the same molecular mechanisms that drive people into drug addiction are behind the compulsion to overeat, pushing people into obesity.

The new study, conducted by Scripps Research Associate Professor Paul J. Kenny and graduate student Paul M. Johnson, was published March 28, 2010 in an advance online edition of the journal *Nature Neuroscience*.

The study's startling findings received widespread publicity after a preliminary abstract was presented at a Society for Neuroscience meeting in Chicago last October [2009]. Articles heralding the new discovery appeared in news publications around the world, focusing on the point obese patients have been making for years—that, like addiction to other substances, junk food binging is extremely difficult to stop.

The study goes significantly further than the abstract, however, demonstrating clearly that in rat models the development of obesity coincides with a progressively deteriorating chemical balance in reward brain circuitries. As these pleasure centers in the brain become less and less responsive, rats quickly develop compulsive overeating habits, consuming larger quantities of high-calorie, high-fat foods until they become obese. The very same changes occur in the brains of rats that overconsume cocaine or heroin, and are thought to play an important role in the development of compulsive drug use.

Kenny, a scientist at Scripps Research's Florida campus, said that the study, which took nearly three years to complete, confirms the "addictive" properties of junk food.

What happens in addiction is lethally simple. . . . The system basically turns on itself, adapting to the new reality of addiction, whether its cocaine or cupcakes.

Rats Fatten Up

The new study, unlike our preliminary abstract, explains what happens in the brain of these animals when they have easy access to high-calorie, high-fat food, said Kenny. "It presents the most thorough and compelling evidence that drug addiction and obesity are based on the same underlying neurobiological mechanisms. In the study, the animals completely lost control over their eating behavior, the primary hallmark of addiction. They continued to overeat even when they anticipated receiving electric shocks, highlighting just how motivated they were to consume the palatable food."

The scientists fed the rats a diet modeled after the type that contributes to human obesity—easy-to-obtain high-calorie, high-fat foods like sausage, bacon, and cheesecake. Soon after the experiments began, the animals began to bulk up dramatically.

"They always went for the worst types of food," Kenny said, "and as a result, they took in twice the calories as the control rats. When we removed the junk food and tried to put them on a nutritious diet—what we called the 'salad bar option'—they simply refused to eat. The change in their diet preference was so great that they basically starved themselves for two weeks after they were cut off from junk food. It was the animals that showed the 'crash' in brain reward circuitries that had the most profound shift in food preference to the palatable, unhealthy diet. These same rats were also those that kept on eating even when they anticipated being shocked."

Lethally Simple

What happens in addiction is lethally simple, Kenny explained. The reward pathways in the brain have been so overstimulated that the system basically turns on itself, adapting to the new reality of addiction, whether its cocaine or cupcakes.

"The body adapts remarkably well to change—and that's the problem," said Kenny. "When the animal overstimulates its brain pleasure centers with highly palatable food, the systems adapt by decreasing their activity. However, now the animal requires constant stimulation from palatable food to avoid entering a persistent state of negative reward."

After showing that obese rats had clear addiction-like food seeking behaviors, Johnson and Kenny next investigated the underlying molecular mechanisms that may explain these changes. They focused on a particular receptor in the brain known to play an important role in vulnerability to drug addiction and obesity—the dopamine D2 receptor. The D2 receptor responds to dopamine, a neurotransmitter that is released in the brain by pleasurable experiences like food or sex or drugs like cocaine. In cocaine abuse, for example, the drug alters the flow of dopamine by blocking its retrieval, flooding the brain and overstimulating the receptors, something that eventually leads to physical changes in the way the brain responds to the drug.

The new study shows that the same thing happens in junk food addiction.

These data are, as far as we know, the strongest support for the idea that overeating of palatable food can become habitual in the same manner and through the same mechanisms as consumption of drugs of abuse.

"These findings confirm what we and many others have suspected," Kenny said, "that overconsumption of highly pleasurable food triggers addiction-like neuroadaptive responses in brain reward circuitries, driving the development of compulsive eating. Common mechanisms may therefore underlie obesity and drug addiction."

Compulsive Overeating

Consistent with common mechanisms explaining addiction and obesity, levels of the D2 dopamine receptors were significantly reduced in the brains of the obese animals, similar to previous reports of what happens in human drug addicts, Kenny noted. Remarkably, when the scientists knocked down the receptor using a specialized virus, the development of addiction-like eating was dramatically accelerated.

This addiction-like behavior happened almost from the moment we knocked down the dopamine receptors, Kenny noted. "The very next day after we provided access to the palatable food, their brains changed into a state that was consistent with an animal that had been overeating for several weeks. The animals also became compulsive in their eating behaviors almost immediately. These data are, as far as we know, the strongest support for the idea that overeating of palatable food can become habitual in the same manner and through the same mechanisms as consumption of drugs of abuse."

13

The Globalization of Fast Food Has Some Benefits

Nishanth Uli

Nishanth Uli wrote this viewpoint for the campus newspaper at Washington University in St. Louis, Missouri, while a student.

While American fast food companies often face criticism for spreading their unhealthy food around the world, the globalization of fast food also has a positive side. Fast food has become a powerful economic and social force and in many countries it serves as a bridge between local cultures and the Western world, the United States in particular. Such "culinary diplomacy" by America's powerhouse fast food ambassadors has led to a positive blending of cultures and understanding that would not have happened otherwise. The global expansion of fast food is less about the homogenization of culture than cultural diffusion.

Fast food moguls like Yum! Brands (operator of Taco Bell and KFC among others), Subway, and McDonald's have been undertaking aggressive expansion efforts across the globe for decades. While these efforts started as smart responses to demand in emerging markets, they have evolved into something much larger. These restaurants provide a mix between good, old-fashioned Americana and the unique local culture. At Chinese KFCs, you can buy Colonel Sanders' patented fried chicken smothered in Peking duck sauce. In India and looking for some Indo-Italian fusion? Just order the Paneer Makhani pie at Pizza Hut. And let's not forget France, where you can find the proud tradition of Gallic cuisine distilled to its purest form in Le Petit McBaguette. This process of cultural diffusion and culinary diplomacy reveals the deep effect that fast food has had on bridging the gaps between different cultures.

Fast food's meteoric rise over the past few decades has reflected the realities of an increasingly globalized world where cultural diffusion and syncretism are the norm.

While its expansion has resulted in increased culinary fusion, fast food has also become an intensely powerful economic and social force. No fast food establishment is more recognizable than McDonald's, the largest chain of restaurants in the world. Founded as a small barbeque joint in 1940, the golden arches can now be found in over 34,000 locations in 122 countries on every continent except Antarctica (although this author firmly believes we'll be eating Chicken McNuggets at the South Pole by 2020). The cultural impact of McDonald's extends far beyond its cuisine. The brand has become an economic and cultural phenomenon in and of itself. The *Economist* regularly publishes a Big Mac index to measure purchasing power parity between nations based on their differing prices for the iconic hamburger. *New York Times* columnist Thomas Friedman, author of *The World Is Flat,* coined the notion of "Golden Arches of Conflict Prevention," which posits that no two countries that have their own McDonald's would go to war with one another. Although presented in a tongue-in-cheek manner, these theories reveal the profound influence that the restaurant chain has had; since its expansion, McDonald's has become a benchmark for globalization and cultural diffusion.

Fast Food Diplomacy

The emergence of a "fast food diplomacy" has engendered a strange interplay of culture and cuisine across the globe.

As fast food's global influence has grown, it has increasingly become the focus of intense criticism and scrutiny. As more and more American fast food franchises open across the world, many see a growing "McDonaldization" of society linked to an idea of American cultural imperialism hell-bent on eradicating the unique cultures and cuisines of the globe. These views have led to a variety of measures against the growing influence of fast food, including, among others, the Italian-based slow food movement, focused on preserving traditional cuisine and promoting environmentally friendly farming. These new initiatives have provided an interesting counterpoint to fast food's rise; as more fast food infiltrates a culture, there seems to be an increasing amount of effort devoted to maintaining that culture's traditional cuisine.

Bridging the Culture Gap

Fast food's meteoric rise over the past few decades has reflected the realities of an increasingly globalized world where cultural diffusion and syncretism are the norm. While McDonald's and Burger King have come to represent America's growing cultural hegemony, the truth is that these brands are less American than ever. They have been forced to adapt to the unique cultures that have taken them in, forcing a radical shift in the way they do business. The problems associated with fast food are undeniable. Increasing obesity, environmental concerns, and limited food supplies are just some of the negative consequences of an increasingly McDonaldized world. However, fast food diplomacy has led to a complex intermingling of culture and cuisine that wouldn't have happened without Ronald McDonald and Colonel Sanders' worldwide advance.

14

Americans' Food Choices Should Not Be Regulated

Michael L. Marlow and Sherzod Abdukadirov

Michael L. Marlow is a professor of economics and distinguished scholar at California Polytechnic State University. Sherzod Abdukadirov is a research fellow in the regulatory studies program at the Mercatus Center at George Mason University in Virginia.

Obesity is a serious health problem but government regulation is not the way to solve it. The booming weight-reduction, health, and fitness industry is proof that the free market is better equipped to provide effective responses to obesity than public policy is. Government paternalism is a flawed approach that relies on interventions that have poor checks and balances for their effectiveness. Personal responsibility is the key to personal change, not regulation that unilaterally imposes change on everyone regardless of whether or not they have a problem. Americans should be free to choose for themselves what to eat and drink, and how much.

Obesity, often defined as having a body mass index 20 percent or more above what is considered "healthy" for a person's height, has recently become our nation's public health obsession. Obesity prevalence in 2007–2008 was 33.8 percent, which represents a 50 percent increase from 1988–1994. Encouragingly, the growth in obesity prevalence appears to be slowing, but a recent article in the *American Journal of Preven-*

tive Medicine predicts that by 2030 42 percent of Americans will be obese and 11 percent will be severely obese, or 100 pounds overweight. The same report, conducted by Duke University and the Centers for Disease Control, estimates an extra $550 billion in health-related costs, along with declining workforce productivity, if that prediction holds true.

Dire predictions often lead to ambitious public policy proposals. The Institute of Medicine (IOM) recently released its 462-page report *Accelerating Progress in Obesity Prevention: Solving the Weight of the Nation.* The IOM, part of the National Academy of Sciences, argues that wide-ranging and systemic changes are required to solve the nation's complex, stubborn obesity problem. Proposed solutions include integrating physical activity into every day life in every way, promoting marketing of what matters for a healthy life, promoting greater availability of healthy foods and beverages, enlisting employers and health care professionals in the fight against obesity, and strengthening schools as the "heart of health." The report concludes that an effective solution requires across-the-board societal change.

Our examination of the obesity issue demonstrates that government intervention is often ineffective in dealing with individual failures, and in some cases is counterproductive.

The IOM offers an extensive list of policies that would effectively steer individuals toward their leaner selves. These include tax preferences for housing developers to build sidewalks and trails, reduction in farm subsidies, changes to zoning laws that make outside exercise easier, requiring primary and secondary schools to provide a daily minimum of 60 minutes of physical activity, banning sugary drinks at schools, and perhaps even taxing soda and other sugar-sweetened beverages.

What the IOM Said

The IOM's motivation for calling upon government is clearly stated on page 117 of the report:

> Theory and empirical data from the field of behavioral eco-- nomics suggest that the majority of physical activity and eating behaviors are routine rather than choices made after deliberation about a set of options.... In such cases, changing the environmental cues or "default choices" to routinely prompt healthier choices could cause favorable (from a public health perspective) shifts in population behavior.

Newspapers quickly responded to the report with headlines informing readers that the IOM concluded that obesity cannot be blamed on a lack of individual willpower. Rather, individuals are unable to truly exercise choice when their options are limited and "biased toward the unhealthy end of the continuum."

This view reflects the growing influence of behavioral economics—a rapidly growing discipline that studies systematic biases of individuals—to justify paternalistic policies. Rising obesity prevalence is viewed as a symptom of individuals pursuing behaviors that conflict with their own best interests. Obesity is considered a reflection of irrational behavior by individuals. Behavioral economists devise "nudges" (soft paternalism) or "shoves" (hard paternalism) that steer individuals toward choices that are more in sync with their best interests. In effect, policymakers are believed able and ready to correct individual departures from rationality.

We believe this paternalistic view warrants closer examination. In particular, we examine the pitfalls of the growing use of behavioral economics to justify government intervention into obesity. Policies are too easy to justify under assumptions that government officials are better informed than the individuals they seek to guide. Our examination of the obesity issue demonstrates that government intervention is often ineffective in dealing with individual failures, and in some cases is counterproductive.

The Case for Paternalism

The traditional paradigm in economics is simply to leave people alone to manage their own lives because they are best able to judge their own welfare. Behavioral economists challenge this view by documenting numerous instances in which individual actions are claimed to have bounded rationality. Not only do individuals make mistakes, but they are believed to repeat the same mistakes under similar conditions. It is not that some people make random irrational choices, but rather that most people deviate from rational decisions in consistent and predictable manners. Choices are thus believed to be systematically biased.

Paternalists ... attempt to selectively punish "bad" behavior by increasing the costs of unhealthy choices.

Systematic biases in human behavior fall into two broad categories. The first includes cognitive biases that prevent people from pursuing actions that improve their welfare. For example, a default option or status-quo bias leads individuals to stick with what they have rather than search for a better alternative. In one natural experiment, a number of Western European countries adopted a policy that assumed deceased individuals to be organ donors by default, instead of the traditional approach in which the deceased previously had to consent explicitly. Under the new regime, individuals still had the right to opt out of being donors, so they still had both choices available to them; the default option simply changed. However, the differences in donation rates between opt-in and opt-out countries were striking: the rate ranged between 4 and 27 percent in opt-in countries, but hovered above 98 percent for most opt-out countries. Changing the default option from opt-in to opt-out led to a remarkable difference in individual decisions.

Self-Control Problems

In the second category, behavioral economists believe individuals suffer from persistent self-control problems. In economic jargon, such individuals are said to suffer from "hyperbolic discounting." That leads them to exhibit time inconsistency about discounting future tradeoffs between the present self and the future self. A smoker may find it hard to quit today, but may nonetheless want to quit "someday" because the benefits of better health outweigh the costs of quitting. The problem is, "someday" never comes; the immediate benefit of continuing smoking today repeatedly outweighs the long-term health benefits of quitting. Consequently, the individual finds it exceedingly difficult to quit smoking. The same logic applies to an obese person trying to stick to a diet or exercise program—"someday" never comes.

The Role of Government

Traditionally, government intervention has been reserved for correcting market failures. The traditional policy toolkit for this is outfitted with two approaches. The first mandates information disclosure to counter information asymmetry. Requiring drug companies to go through testing processes and food companies to disclose calorie counts are examples of such interventions. The second approach increases the costs of "bad" behavior often associated with negative externalities, either through command-and-control regulation, penalties, or taxes. Cigarette taxes and mandatory pollution control devices are examples of this form of intervention.

Paternalists concerned about obesity have proposed using both approaches. Governments have required food producers and servers to disclose calorie counts, sugar and fat contents, and other information to steer consumers toward healthier choices. In doing this, policymakers assume consumers are poorly informed and that fuller disclosure of nutritional information will remedy the problem. Legislation requiring restaurants to print calorie counts of their meals on their menus was first introduced at the local government level in New York City and King County, Washington, and is now proposed on the federal level. Concerning the second, hard-paternalist form of intervention, New York became the first major city to ban trans-fats in 2006, soon followed by Philadelphia. California followed suit by a partial ban on trans-fats at the state level. Paternalists thus attempt to selectively punish "bad" behavior by increasing the costs of unhealthy choices, similar to policies aimed at correcting negative externalities such as pollution. Some governments plan to press further by raising taxes on, or even banning, various unhealthy foods.

It is not surprising that recent interventions are not very effective when they simply provide citizens with information that they already know.

We argue that it is inappropriate for these nutrition activists to borrow claims that markets suffer from information asymmetries or negative externalities and then presume such problems also influence individual behavior. Most obese individuals know they are heavy, and that many of the foods they eat are high-calorie. They also face the stigma often linked to obesity. They hardly need the government to give them additional incentives to lose weight. People aware of their mistakes also have strong incentives to correct them. This is an important point because interventions focusing on health risks of obesity may provide minimal new information and steer few people toward losing weight.

Adults Know the Risks

Studies indicate that adults recognize various personal health risks associated with obesity. [Eric A.] Finkelstein et al. conducted a survey of 1,130 U.S. adults to test whether overweight and obese individuals recognize that they are at greater risk of obesity-related diseases and premature mortality. They found that obese (overweight) adults forecast life expectancies 3.9 (2.4) years shorter than those of normal-weight adults. Excess weight was associated with greater self-perceived risk of developing diabetes, cancer, heart disease, and stroke. The authors concluded that mortality predictions generated from the survey were "reasonably close" to those generated from actual life tables for U.S. adults.

Thus it is not surprising that recent interventions are not very effective when they simply provide citizens with information that they already know. A study of New York City's 2008 law on posting calories in restaurant chains examined how menu calorie labels influenced fast food choices. While 28 percent of patrons in New York said the information influenced their choices, researchers could not detect a change in calories purchased after the law. A similar conclusion was reached in a study of a mandatory menu-labeling regulation requiring all restaurant chains with 15 or more locations to disclose calorie information in King County, Washington. [Bryan] Bollinger et al. studied the impact of mandatory calorie posting on consumers' purchase decisions at Starbucks. While average calories per transaction fell by 6 percent, the effect was almost entirely related to changes in consumers' food rather than drink choices. Starbucks is well known for high-calorie coffee drinks loaded with cream, yet mandatory calorie disclosure apparently did little to avert consumer taste for those specialties.

It would seem that consumers were either well informed prior to regulations or chose to ignore new information provided to them. Well-informed consumers indicate no economic justification for intervention. However, paternalists might still object and push for even stronger measures aimed at correcting what they view as repeated mistakes by consumers who insist on not changing eating and drinking patterns that paternalists believe are causes of obesity. The paternalists apparently believe that curtailing consumption is the only rational response to their regulations, and thus unchanged behavior indicates continued irrationality.

Recent evidence also questions interventions that attempt to steer the obese away from "junk food."

The Obesity Wage Penalty

It is well known that the obese earn less than the non-obese. [Charles L.] Baum and [William F.] Ford concluded that both men and women experienced a persistent obesity wage penalty over the first two decades of their careers. [John] Cawley found that obese white females earned 11.2 percent lower wages than their non-obese counterparts. A difference in weight of roughly 65 pounds was associated with a difference in wages of 9 percent. [Jay] Bhattacharya and [M. Kate] Bundorf found that cash wages for obese workers were lower than those for non-obese workers because the cost to employers of providing health insurance for these workers was higher. Obese workers with employer-sponsored health insurance thus paid for their greater medical costs by receiving lower cash wages than were paid to non-obese workers.

Business owners understand that healthy employees are more productive, miss fewer work days, and reduce health insurance costs. One study has estimated that higher job absenteeism associated with obesity costs $4.3 billion annually in the United States. A study by the Johnson and Johnson family of companies found that its workplace health promotion program led to an average annual per-employee savings of $565 (in 2009 dollars), or about $1.88–$3.92 for every dollar spent.

In a meta-analysis of the literature on cost savings associated with such programs, [Katherine] Baicker et al. found that medical costs fall by about $3.27 for every dollar spent on wellness programs and that absenteeism costs fall by about $2.73 for every dollar spent.

Recent evidence also questions interventions that attempt to steer the obese away from "junk food." [Jennifer] Van Hook and [Claire E.] Altman concluded that children with access to junk food (e.g., soft drinks, candy bars, potato chips) were no heavier than those without. The study followed nearly 20,000 students from kindergarten through the eighth grade in 1,000 public and private schools and found that in the eighth grade, 35.5 percent of kids in schools with junk food were overweight, while 34.8 percent of those in schools without it were overweight. Food sales within schools were, on average, unrelated to obesity, thus raising questions about school-based interventions aimed at reducing childhood obesity.

Research also demonstrates that tax hikes on alcohol and tobacco mostly decrease consumption by light users instead of heavy users. This suggests that raising taxes on junk food will mostly cause people without problems to cut back their consumption, while people with problems will simply pay higher taxes. Taxes steer the elastic consumers, more than inelastic, away from taxed products and thus exert little to no behavioral effect on the inelastic consumers, such as obese citizens, targeted by government. Higher taxes and/or bans will be the course of action when paternalists come to realize their past interventions have not met their predictions.

The Diet Industry

The demand for solutions to America's obesity problem is evidenced by the market for diet books, health foods, weight loss centers, exercise equipment, athletic clubs, and other methods people use to control their weight. Many hotel chains offer memberships to their fitness facilities to non-residents for a monthly fee. Diet sodas and low-calorie meals can be purchased at countless independent and chain eateries. Between 1987 and 2004, 35,272 new food products labeled "low fat" or "no fat" were introduced into the U.S. food market, leading U.S. Department of Agriculture researchers to conclude that there is no market failure in healthy food and beverage choices. Sales of Diet Coke overtook those of Pepsi-Cola for the first time in 2010, making it the second most popular carbonated soft drink in the United States. The Subway sandwich chain, known for healthier fare, recently surpassed McDonald's Corp. as the world's largest restaurant chain measured in number of locations.

An active private market in providing healthy choices again suggests that paternalists overstate their case for intervention. By ignoring the market's attempts to deal with obesity, paternalists gain great latitude to overstate the effectiveness of their interventions as they apparently believe that without government we are unlikely to see any improvement in obesity prevalence.

Good intentions aside, we should be skeptical of the notion that new interventions will somehow lower obesity when research has yet to prove that past programs have (unintentionally) not promoted obesity.

Systematic Biases and Bad Information

Behavioral economists inexplicably assume that individuals who supposedly act irrationally in their private choices turn into paragons of rationality when they become bureaucrats. But in fact, [F.H.] Buckley points out that policymakers are likely to suffer from hindsight bias. To a paternalist looking back at an accident after the fact, a low-probability accident may look like a certainty. This is part of a more general egocentric bias in which paternalists greatly overestimate their abilities.

In addition to systematic biases, paternalistic policymakers suffer from imperfect information. Policymakers make choices when evidence is ambiguous and does not favor any given option. In one example, the U.S. Food and Drug Administration recently proposed a regulation that would require vending machines to display the calorie content of vended items. Its reasoning for the proposed rule is illuminating. The FDA acknowledged that the vending market is highly competitive and thus if consumers demanded calorie count displays, the market would oblige. So by the agency's own admission, there is no market failure in calorie count information. Providing information to consumers they already know and/or disregard is unlikely to benefit them, but costs society an estimated $24.5 million each year.

Efficacy of Nutritional Labeling Is in Doubt

Effectiveness of nutritional labeling regulation is also subject to great debate. Private companies have been experimenting with various types of nutritional labeling. Studies show that they are far more effective in communicating health information to customers than government programs. Stringent government regulation that prescribes particular methods of disclosure constrains private experimentation. The end result is that anti-obesity regulation may reduce the number of innovative solutions that could help individuals control their weight. Unfortunately, more effective and cheaper solutions may simply remain undiscovered and never implemented to help remedy the problem that has been targeted by the regulator.

Paternalistic policies also open up new areas of influence to special interests and lobbyists. Affected industries have strong incentives to shape policy to their own benefit. Yet, paternalists often forget that policymaking itself is a political process given their implicit assumptions that policies are crafted by benevolent, perfectly rational, and fully informed bureaucrats. Rather, policies result from contentious political processes in which competing interests collide over a range of issues. The final compromise may be far from the most efficient course of action (even if it were available).

There is also little evidence that previous government intervention has lowered obesity among the poor. The USDA concludes that, despite many low-income individuals being both obese and recipients of one or more food assistance programs, the research literature does not show that programs have lowered obesity. [Jay L.] Zagorsky and [Patricia K.] Smith find that the typical female food stamp participant's body mass index is significantly more than someone with the same socioeconomic characteristics who is not in the program. For the average American woman, who is 5 ft., 4 in. tall, this means an increase in weight of 5.8 pounds. Good intentions aside, we should be skeptical of the notion that new interventions will somehow lower obesity when research has yet to prove that past programs have (unintentionally) not promoted obesity.

Regulations Are Not the Answer

Obesity is a serious health problem. This article demonstrates that using behavioral economics to guide regulations is both misguided and can be counterproductive to obese and non-obese citizens alike.

Somewhat lost in the public health debate is that people who are aware that they are overweight also experience strong incentives to undertake their own strategies to lose weight. Obese individuals know they are heavy and also suffer the stigma often linked to obesity. Employers have incentives to push their employees to lose weight. A growing demand for weight reduction is evidenced by the ever-growing market for diet books, health foods, weight loss centers, exercise equipment, athletic clubs, and other methods people use to control their weight.

Paternalists ignore the market attempts to deal with obesity since it offers them great latitude to overstate the effectiveness of their interventions. They apparently believe that, without government, we are unlikely to see any improvement in obesity prevalence. Unfortunately, regulators are tempted to turn to "harder" paternalism when they realize past interventions were ineffective.

Substituting government responsibility for personal responsibility over weight has other downsides. Regulators choose one-size-fits-all interventions that ignore the fact that not all obese individuals suffer from the same problems. Regulators also cannot differentiate between those with and without weight problems, as they impose regulations on all citizens. Interventions also crowd out market solutions that arise as firms compete with each other by innovating and providing customers a wide variety of products and services that best serve their needs. Regulation involves government officials picking one strategy over others without having to win customers within a competitive marketplace. Regulation thus can retard innovation in the search for better solutions. Of course, even if paternalists knew what the "right" policies are, it is unlikely that these policies would make it through the political process unscathed, as special interests and lawmakers become involved.

Organizations to Contact

The editors have compiled the following list of organizations concerned with the issues debated in this book. The descriptions are derived from materials provided by the organizations. All have publications or information available for interested readers. The list was compiled on the date of publication of the present volume; names, addresses, phone and fax numbers, and e-mail and Internet addresses may change. Be aware that many organizations take several weeks or longer to respond to inquiries, so allow as much time as possible.

American Diabetes Association (ADA)
1701 North Beauregard St., Alexandria, VA   22311
(800) 342-2383
e-mail: askADA@diabetes.org
website: www.diabetes.org

The American Diabetes Association (ADA) is a nonprofit health advocacy organization that works to prevent and cure diabetes, an obesity-related disease. Since food and good nutrition are critical to managing diabetes, the ADA educates people about disease prevention and changing their diet and lifestyle. As a part of its program, the ADA provides a guide to eating out and tips for how to order healthier items while dining at restaurants and fast food establishments. Search the term "fast food" to access more than 1,400 articles, tips, profiles, and recipes related to fast food on the ADA website.

Center for Science in the Public Interest (CSPI)
1875 Connecticut Ave. NW, #300
Washington, DC   20009-5728
(202) 332-9110
e-mail: cspi@cspinet.org
website: www.cspinet.org

Formed in 1971, the Center for Science in the Public Interest (CSPI) is a nonprofit education and consumer advocacy organization dedicated to fighting for government food policies and corporate practices that promote healthy diets. CSPI also works to prevent deceptive marketing and ensure that science is used for public welfare. It publishes *Nutrition Action Health-letter*, the most widely circulated health newsletter in North America. The organization's website includes dozens of news articles, reports, press releases, and other publications related to fast food, including ratings of the best and worst fast food meals with respect to nutrition.

Centers for Disease Control and Prevention (CDC), Division of Nutrition, Physical Activity, and Obesity (DNPAO)

1600 Clifton Rd., Atlanta, GA   30333
(800) 232-4636
e-mail: cdcinfo@cdc.gov
website: www.cdc.gov/nccdphp/dnpa

The Centers for Disease Control and Prevention (CDC) is part of the National Institutes of Health (NIH), Department of Health and Human Services (DHHS). Its Division of Nutrition, Physical Activity, and Obesity (DNPAO) has three focus areas: nutrition, physical activity, and obesity. The DNPAO addresses the role of nutrition and physical activity in improving the public's health. DNPAO activities include health promotion, research, training, and education. The DNPAO maintains an archive of articles on its website, many of which are about the relationship between obesity and fast food.

Children's Food and Beverage Advertising Initiative

4200 Wilson Blvd, Suite 800, Arlington, VA   22203-1838
(703) 276-0100
website: www.bbb.org/council/the-national-partner-program
/national-advertising-review-services/childrens-food-and
-beverage-advertising-initiative

The Children's Food and Beverage Advertising Initiative was launched by the Council of Better Business Bureaus (BBBs) in November 2006 to give companies that advertise food and beverages to children a transparent and accountable advertising regulation tool. The group's mission is to shift the focus of advertisements directed to children under twelve to encourage healthier diet choices. Participating companies must have standards consistent with US Department of Agriculture and other scientific and government organizations, and all companies that register with the Initiative are monitored by the BBB to ensure compliance. The Initiative's website features statements and pledges from participating companies, including fast food giants such as Burger King and McDonald's.

Food Marketing Institute (FMI)
2345 Crystal Dr., Suite 800, Arlington, VA   22202
(202) 452-8444 • fax: (202) 429-4519
website: www.fmi.org

The Food Marketing Institute (FMI) conducts programs in public affairs, food safety, research, education, and industry relations on behalf of food retailers and wholesalers in the United States and around the globe. FMI provides leadership and advocacy for the food distribution industry as it works to meet customers' changing needs. The Health and Wellness section of the organization's website provides information about nutrition, nutrition labeling, and obesity.

Food Research and Action Center (FRAC)
1200 18th St. NW, Suite 400, Washington, DC   20036
(202) 986-2200 • fax: (202) 986-2525
e-mail: jadach@frac.org
website: www.frac.org

The Food Research and Action Center (FRAC) is the leading national nonprofit organization working to improve public policies and public-private partnerships to eradicate hunger and under-nutrition in the United States. FRAC serves as a watchdog of regulations and policies affecting the poor, and it conducts public information campaigns to ensure that children of low-income families receive healthy and nutritious food. The "Fighting Obesity and Hunger" section of the group's website includes a wide variety of information about the risk factors for obesity or under-nourishment, including poverty, and the availability of fresh versus convenience foods.

National Council of Chain Restaurants (NCCR)
325 7th St. NW, Suite 1100, Washington, DC   20004
(202) 626-8189
website: www.nccr.net

The National Council of Chain Restaurants (NCCR) is a division of the National Retail Federation and is the national trade association that represents the chain restaurant industry. The NCCR works to advance public policy that serves the interests of chain restaurants and the three million people they employ. The organization's website provides up-to-date industry news; links to government-relations resources; a Legislative Action Center where visitors can research legislation and learn how to work with Congress; and for members of the site, access to *NCCR Highlights Newsletter*.

National Restaurant Association
2055 L St. NW, Suite 700, Washington, DC   20036
(202) 331-5900
website: www.restaurant.org

The National Restaurant Association represents and promotes America's $566 billion restaurant business. It promotes a pro-restaurant agenda and argues on behalf of the restaurant industry before Congress and federal regulatory agencies and works to battle anti-restaurant initiatives. Reports, publications, press releases, and research about important topics affecting the food industry can all be found on its website, including a wide variety of information about the "quick-serve" or fast food restaurant industry.

The Obesity Society (TOS)
8757 Georgia Ave., Suite 1320, Silver Spring, MD   20910
(301) 563-6526 • fax: (301) 563-6595
website: www.obesity.org

The Obesity Society (TOS) is the leading scientific organization dedicated to the study of obesity and its health effects. Its researchers seek to understand the causes and treatment of obesity while also keeping the medical community informed of the latest advances in research. It publishes the journal *Obesity*, and several newsletters and reports found on its website discuss the link between fast food and obesity. The Obesity Society supports mandatory calorie counts and nutritional labeling for fast food restaurants.

US Department of Agriculture (USDA),
Food and Nutrition Service (FNS)
1400 Independence Ave. SW, Washington, DC   20250
(202) 720-2791
website: www.usda.gov

The Food and Nutrition Service (FNS) is an agency of the US Department of Agriculture (USDA) that is responsible for administering the nation's domestic nutrition assistance programs. It provides prepared meals, food assistance, and nutrition education materials to one in five Americans. The agency encourages children and teens to follow its dietary guidelines and a guide for healthy restaurant eating is available from the FNS website.

US Food and Drug Administration (FDA)
10903 New Hampshire Ave., Silver Spring, MD   20993
(888) 463-6332
e-mail: webmail@oc.fda.gov
website: www.fda.gov

The US Food and Drug Administration (FDA) is a public health agency charged with protecting American consumers by enforcing the Federal Food, Drug, and Cosmetic Act and several related public health laws. The FDA sends investigators and inspectors into the field to ensure that the country's almost 95,000 FDA-regulated businesses are compliant. Its publications include government documents, reports, fact sheets, and press announcements. It also provides food labeling guidance and regulatory information for restaurants on its website. Of particular note is the publication titled "Overview of FDA Proposed Labeling Requirements for Restaurants, Similar

Fast Food

Retail Food Establishments and Vending Machines," which explains the rules about calorie counts and nutrition information on fast food restaurant menus.

Bibliography

Books

Paul Barron	*The Chipotle Effect: The Changing Landscape of the American Social Consumer and How Fast Casual Is Impacting the Future of Restaurants.* Boca Raton, FL: Transmedia, 2012.
Laura Dawes	*Childhood Obesity in America: Biography of an Epidemic.* Boston: Harvard University Press, 2014.
David G. Hogan	*Selling 'em by the Sack: White Castle and the Creation of American Food.* New York: New York University Press, 1999.
Ray Kroc	*Grinding It Out: The Making of McDonald's.* New York: St Martin's, 1992.
Michael Moss	*Salt, Sugar, Fat: How the Food Giants Hooked Us.* New York: Random House, 2013.
Marion Nestle	*Food Politics: How the Food Industry Influences Nutrition and Health.* Berkeley: University of California Press, 2013.
Josh Ozersky	*Colonel Sanders and the American Dream.* Austin: University of Texas Press, 2012.

Participant Media *Food Inc.: How Industrial Food Is*
and Karl Weber   *Making Us Sicker, Fatter, and*
                  Poorer—And What You Can Do About
                  It. New York: PublicAffairs, 2009.

Stacy Perman   *In-N-Out Burger: A*
                  Behind-the-Counter Look at the
                  Fast-Food Chain That Breaks All the
                  Rules. New York: Harper Business,
                  2010.

Michael Pollan   *The Omnivore's Dilemma: A Natural*
                  History of Four Meals. New York:
                  Penguin, 2007.

Eric Schlosser   *Fast Food Nation: The Dark Side of*
                  the All-American Meal. Boston:
                  Mariner, 2012.

Andrew F. Smith   *Encyclopedia of Junk Food and Fast*
                  Food. Westport, CT: Greenwood,
                  2006.

Morgan Spurlock   *Don't Eat This Book: Fast Food and*
                  the Supersizing of America. Berkeley,
                  CA: Berkeley Trade, 2006.

Charles Wilson   *Chew on This: Everything You Don't*
and Eric Schlosser *Want to Know About Fast Food.*
                  Boston: Houghton Mifflin, 2007.

Periodicals and Internet Sources

Toby Amidor   "Has Fast Food Become Healthier?,"
                  U.S. News & World Report, October
                  21, 2013.

Judy Bankman
and Ross Miranti

"Junk Food Marketing Makes Big Moves in Developing Countries," Civil Eats, October 2, 2013. http:// civileats.com.

David Barboza

"Fast Food Industry Zeroes in on Children," *New York Times*, August 5, 2003.

Patrick Basham
and John Luik

"A Happy Meal Ban Is Nothing to Smile About," *Spiked*, November 9, 2010. www.spiked-online.com.

Patrick Basham
and John Luik

"Are You Dying for a Fix of Burger and Chips?," *Spiked*, April 6, 2010. www.spiked-online.com.

Jillian Berman

"America's Terrible Fast Food Pay Has Gone Global, and Workers Are Fighting Back," *Huffington Post*, May 15, 2014. www.huffingtonpost.com.

Sharon Bernstein

"Fast-Food Industry Is Quietly Defeating Happy Meal Bans," *Los Angeles Times*, May 18, 2011.

Mark Bittman

"Yes, Healthful Fast Food Is Possible. But Edible?," *New York Times*, April 3, 2013.

Kelly Brownell

"Are Children Prey for Fast Food Companies?," *Atlantic*, November 8, 2010.

Kiera Butler

"Fast Food's Litter Legacy," *Mother Jones*, June 27, 2011.

Center for Science in the Public Interest	"Research Review: Effects of Eating Out on Nutrition and Body Weight," 2008. www.cspinet.org.
Centers for Disease Control and Prevention	"Childhood Obesity," 2008. www.cdc.gov.
Jeanie Lerche Davis	"Fast Food Creates Fat Kids: Kids Can Gain Six Pounds a Year from Fast Food," *Web MD Health News*, January 5, 2004. www.webmd.com.
Kathleen Doheny	"Fast Food Not Major Culprit in Kids' Obesity: Study," HealthDay, January 17, 2014. http://consumer.healthday.com.
Kathleen Doheny	"Many People Ignore, Miss Calorie Counts on Fast-Food Menus: Survey," HealthDay, November 15, 2013. http://consumer.healthday.com.
Josh Eidelson	"McDonald's Ex-Managers Sound Off to Salon: Non-Existent Breaks and Illegal Overtime," *Salon*, April 1, 2014. www.salon.com.
Brian Elbel, J. Gyamfi, and R. Kersh	"Child and Adolescent Fast Food Choice and the Influence of Calorie Labeling: A Natural Experiment," National Center for Biotechnology Information, February 15, 2011. www.ncbi.nlm.nih.gov.
Emily Jane Fox	"Fast Food Worker: Protest Didn't Cost Me Pay," CNNMoney, December 6, 2013. http://money.cnn.com.

David H. Freedman	"How Junk Food Can End Obesity," *Atlantic*, June 19, 2013.
Andrea Freeman	"Fast Food: Oppression Through Poor Nutrition," *California Law Review*, December 31, 2007.
Steven Greenhouse	"McDonald's Workers File Wage Suits in Three States," *New York Times*, March 13, 2014.
Alison Griswold	"Here's Why the Fast-Food Breakfast Wars Are Raging," *Slate*, April 2, 2014. www.slate.com.
Tiffany Hsu	"Nearly 90% of Fast-Food Workers Allege Wage Theft, Survey Finds," *Los Angeles Times*, April 1, 2014.
Rex Huppke	"Tribune Columnist Rex Huppke Examines Both Sides of the Latest Debate on Increasing the Federal Minimum Wage in America," *Chicago Tribune*, March 24, 2014.
Mark Hyman	"Why Quick, Cheap Food Is Actually More Expensive," *Huffington Post*, August 14, 2010. www.huffingtonpost.com.
Sarah Jaffe	"McJobs Should Pay, Too: Inside Fast-Food Workers' Historic Protest for Living Wages," *Atlantic*, November 29, 2012.
Mary Clare Jalonick	"Menu Labeling Law: Calorie Counts Are a 'Thorny' Issue, FDA Head Says," *Huffington Post*, March 12, 2013. www.huffingtonpost.com.

Randy James   "A Brief History of McDonald's Abroad," *Time*, October 28, 2009.

Frederik Joelving   "Ban Fast Food Ads on TV: US Doctors," Reuters, June 27, 2011. www.reuters.com.

Sebastian Joseph   "Fast Food Brands Face Calls for Watershed Ad Ban," *Marketing Week*, March 21, 2014.

Roxanne Khamsi   "Fast Food Branding Makes Children Prefer Happy Meals," *New Scientist*, August 6, 2007.

Kristin Kirkpatrick   "Fast Food's Immediate Damage to Your Health," *Huffington Post*, December 3, 2012. www.huffingtonpost.com.

Lorinda Klein   "Mandatory Calorie Postings at Fast-Food Chains Often Ignored or Unseen, Does Not Influence Food Choice," NYU Langone Medical Center/New York University School of Medicine, November 15, 2013. www.eurekalert.org.

Matthew Kling and Ian Hough   "The American Carbon Footprint—Understanding and Reducing Your Food's Impact on Climate Change," Brighter Planet, 2010. www.kohalacenter.org.

Dana Liebelson   "McDonald's Definition of 'Sustainable': Brought to You by the Beef Industry," *Mother Jones*, March 20, 2014.

Barry Marcus   "Reasons Why Fast Food Restaurants
                        Are Responsible for America's
                        Obesity Epidemic," Culinary Arts
                        360, June 16, 2009.
                        www.culinaryarts360.com.

Claire McCarthy   "Passing the Buck? Parental
                        Responsibility vs. Fast Food Giants,"
                        Thriving, May 25, 2010.
                        http://childrenshospitalblog.org.

Ken McGuffin   "Exposure to Fast Food Influences
                        Our Everyday Psychology and
                        Behavior," *Medical News Today*,
                        March 26, 2010. www.medicalnews
                        today.com.

Meredith Melnick   "Calorie Counts on Menus:
                        Apparently, Nobody Cares," *Time*,
                        February 16, 2011.

Meredith Melnick   "Study: Fast-Food Ads Target Kids
                        with Unhealthy Food, and It Works,"
                        Time, November 8, 2010.

Joseph Mercola   "What Is in Fast Food? A Newly
                        Discovered Reason to Avoid Fast
                        Food," *Huffington Post*, December 29,
                        2010. www.huffingtonpost.com.

New York Times   "Happy Meals, Unhappy Workers,"
                        March 13, 2014.

Tom Philpott   "In Praise of Fast Food," *Grist*,
                        November 6, 2010. http://grist.org.

Tom Philpott   "Why the *Atlantic*'s Defense of Junk
                        Food Fails," *Mother Jones*, June 26,
                        2013.

J.M. Poti, K.J. Duffey, and B.M. Popkin	"The Association of Fast Food Consumption with Poor Dietary Outcomes and Obesity Among Children: Is It the Fast Food or the Remainder of Diet?," *American Journal of Clinical Nutrition*, January 2014.
Benjamin Radford	"Junk Food Studies Ignore Parent Responsibility," *Discovery*, November 16, 2010. http://news.discovery.com.
Reuters	"Lack of Regulation of Fast Food Fueling Obesity Epidemic, Study Says," February 3, 2014. www.reuters.com.
Peter Salisbury	"The Globalization of 'Fast Food,' Behind the Brand: McDonald's," Global Research, May 1, 2014. www.globalresearch.ca.
Alana Semuels	"Rousing Workers to Seek Higher Wages," *Los Angeles Times*, September 10, 2013.
Kim Severson	"Los Angeles Stages a Fast Food Intervention," *Los Angeles Times*, August 13, 2008.
Stephen Smith	"Food, Fun—and Fat: The Battle to Shrink the Waistlines of America's Children Focuses Increasingly on How Food Is Marketed, Including the Use of Toys as Lures," *Boston Globe*, July 19, 2010.

Tracy A. Stanciel	"McDonald's Isn't Making Your Kid Fat, but Maybe You Are!," Chicago Now, April 13, 2012. www.chicago now.com.
Linda Thrasybule	"Junk Food Might Not Be Addictive, After All," MyHealthNewsDaily, March 26, 2013. www.livescience .com.
Ben Tracy	"Fast Food Restaurants Not Fighting Child Obesity," CBS News, November 9, 2010. www.cbsnews.com.
Sonia van Gilder Cooke	"Why Going Green Can Mean Big Money for Fast-Food Chains," *Time*, April 9, 2012.
Voice of Liberty	"In Fast Food, There's No Such Thing as a Free Lunch," June 2013. http://thevoiceofliberty.us.
Angelo Young	"Fast Food Workers Lawsuits Claim Relationship Between Franchiser and Corporate Parent Is Closer than It Seems," *International Business Times*, March 13, 2014.
Paul Zollinger-Read	"Is It Time Fast Food Restaurants Became More Responsible?," *Guardian*, July 5, 2013.

Index

University of Texas Southwestern
  Medical Center, 31
US Department of Agriculture
  (USDA), 8, 37, 91, 93
US Department of Health, 61
US Food and Drug Administra-
  tion (FDA), 92

V

Vegetarian options, 23–24

W

Wage theft concerns, 67–68
Weintraub, Daniel, 53, 55
Wendy's fast food, 26, 31

White Oak Pastures, 18
Wolf, Barney, 16–24
Worker impact from fast food, 14
The World Is Flat (Friedman), 80
Wortman, Megan, 22

X

Xoco, 20

Y

Yale Rudd Center for Food Policy
  & Obesity, 39–40
Yeah! Burger, 17, 21

19.46

CPSIA information can be obtained
at www.ICGtesting.com
Printed in the USA
FFOW02n0416180615
14412FF

9 780737 771664